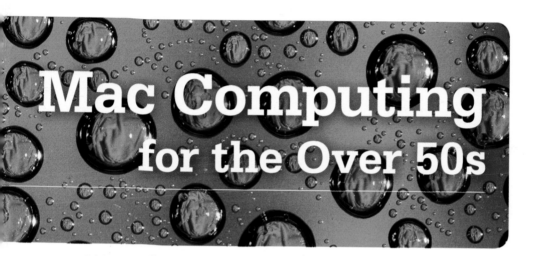

Mac Computing
for the Over 50s

Prentice Hall
is an imprint of

PEARSON

Harlow, England • London • New York • Boston • San Francisco • Toronto • Sydney • Singapore • Hong Kong
Tokyo • Seoul • Taipei • New Delhi • Cape Town • Madrid • Mexico City • Amsterdam • Munich • Paris • Milan

PEARSON EDUCATION LIMITED

Edinburgh Gate
Harlow CM20 2JE
Tel: +44 (0)1279 623623
Fax: +44 (0)1279 431059
Website: www.pearson.com/uk

First published in Great Britain in 2012

ISBN: 978-0-273-76108-2

British Library Cataloguing-in-Publication Data
A catalogue record for this book is available from the British Library

Library of Congress Cataloging-in-Publication Data
A catalog record for this book is available from the Library of Congress

10 9 8 7 6 5 4 3 2 1
15 14 13 12 11

Designed by pentacorbig, High Wycombe
Cover image Magicinfoto, 2011. Used under licence from Shutterstock.com
Typeset in 11/14 pt ITC Stone Sans by 30
Printed and bound by Rotolito Lombarda, Italy

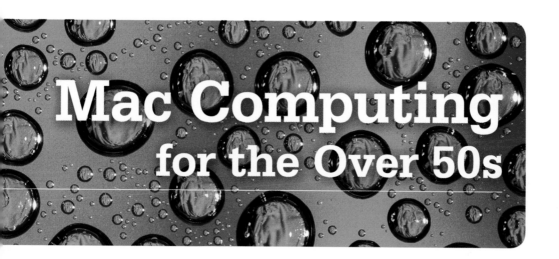

Mac Computing
for the Over 50s

in **Simple** steps

Joli Ballew

Use your computer with confidence

Get to grips with practical computing tasks with minimal time, fuss and bother.

In Simple Steps guides guarantee immediate results. They tell you everything you need to know on a specific application; from the most essential tasks to master, to every activity you'll want to accomplish, through to solving the most common problems you'll encounter.

Helpful features

To build your confidence and help you to get the most out of your computer, practical hints, tips and shortcuts feature on every page:

 ALERT: Explains and provides practical solutions to the most commonly encountered problems

 HOT TIP: Time and effort saving shortcuts

 SEE ALSO: Points you to other related tasks and information

 DID YOU KNOW? Additional features to explore

WHAT DOES THIS MEAN?
Jargon and technical terms explained in plain English

Practical. Simple. Fast.

Dedication:

For my faithful readers who have found their way into the world of computing via a Mac; welcome!

Author's acknowledgements:

I want to thank Steve Temblett for once again choosing me to write another *In Simple Steps* book. I've lost count, but I think we're nearing a dozen or so. I really like writing these books, and I especially enjoy writing for my contemporaries, my over-50s' audience. I thank you for purchasing this book and placing your trust in me to teach you about your Mac. I'd also like to thank my copyeditors, technical editors, layout technicians and others involved in the book-writing process. These include Steve Temblett, Natasha Whelan, Viv Church and the rest of the gang. All of these people make sure that the text is accurate, that the grammar is correct, and that the images are placed properly in the text, among other things. I could not do it without them.

I would also like to thank my agent, Neil Salkind, Ph.D., from the Salkind Literary Agency. We've been together for a decade and during that time we've managed to publish 40+ books together. Over the years, we've become friends, too. And finally, I'd like to acknowledge my family, including my dad, my daughter Jennifer, her husband Andrew, and my partner Cosmo. They are very supportive of me and of my work and I appreciate and love them dearly.

Contents at a glance

Contents

2 Customise your Mac

3 Work with windows, files and folders

4 Explore applications

7 Use Mail, iCal and Address Book

8 Upload, view and manage pictures

9 Play, manage and obtain media

10 Secure and maintain your Mac

11 Use and configure assistive technologies

Top 10 Mac Problems Solved

Top 10 Mac Tips

Tip 1: Find anything with Spotlight Search

Sometimes, browsing through the folders in the Finder or on the Desktop can become cumbersome. An alternative to browsing is to search. The Finder window contains a Spotlight Search box that you can use to search for a file, application or other item by name. You can also access a Search window from the Menu bar.

1 Locate any Spotlight Search window.

2 Type what you're looking for.

3 Click the item to open it.

🔥 **HOT TIP:** When you open a picture or file, you can click the red X in the top left corner of the window to close it.

❓ **DID YOU KNOW?**

If you receive an error and are prompted to 'Fix Alias', do so. An alias is a shortcut, and often, shortcuts can become 'orphaned' and no longer be associated with a particular file.

Tip 2: Make aliases for the Desktop

An alias, in Mac-speak, is a shortcut to something. You can create aliases for folders and applications (among other things) and place those aliases on the Desktop to make them easier to open. For instance, you can create an alias for the Movies folder, so you can access it from the Desktop instead of having to open the Finder to get to it.

1 Open Finder from the Dock.

2 Locate any item you'd like to create an alias for and click it once.

3 On the keyboard, click Command + L. (Alternatively, you could click the File menu and click Make Alias.)

4 Drag the alias to the Desktop.

? DID YOU KNOW?
You can create aliases for applications, documents, PDF files, images and folders, among other things.

🔥 HOT TIP: You can drag any alias to the Trash without fear of losing any data. Aliases are simply shortcuts to data stored elsewhere and do not, in themselves, hold any actual data.

? DID YOU KNOW?
You can drag any alias to the Dock and drop it there if you need an alias but don't want to clutter up your Desktop with icons.

Tip 3: Keep notes on your computer Desktop with Stickies

As you get older, you may find yourself writing more and more notes about things you need to do, pick up or purchase. These notes can be easily misplaced, though. Stickies solves that problem by letting you make notes right on your Mac and save them to the Desktop. You can even print them and take them with you, if necessary.

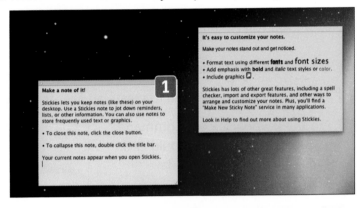

1 From the Finder's Application window, open Stickies. Read what's offered.

2 Verify Stickies is showing on the Menu bar and click File>New Note.

3 Type your note.

4 Click Font>Show Fonts. If desired, choose a new Font Size.

5 To quit Stickies, click Stickies>Quit Stickies.

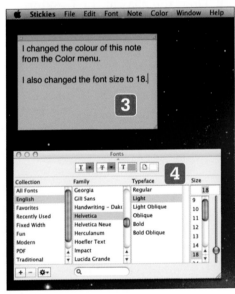

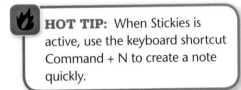

HOT TIP: When Stickies is active, use the keyboard shortcut Command + N to create a note quickly.

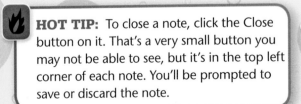

HOT TIP: To close a note, click the Close button on it. That's a very small button you may not be able to see, but it's in the top left corner of each note. You'll be prompted to save or discard the note.

ALERT: If, in step 3, Stickies is not showing on the Menu bar, click any note to make the application active.

Tip 4: Join a public, wireless network

When you take your laptop to a public place such as a coffee shop, pub, hotel, or the like, you may find that the establishment offers free Wi-Fi that enables you to connect to the Internet. These types of networks are called 'hotspots' and are generally unsecured, meaning they do not require you to input a password.

1 Get within range of a free, unsecured Wi-Fi network.

2 When you see a prompt about joining that network, click it to join.

3 If you do not see a prompt:

    a. Open System Preferences and click Network.

    b. Click AirPort.

    c. If Airport is turned off, turn it on.

    d. If Ask to join new networks is not enabled, enable it.

    e. If prompted to apply the changes, click Apply.

    f. When you see the prompt to join the network, select it.

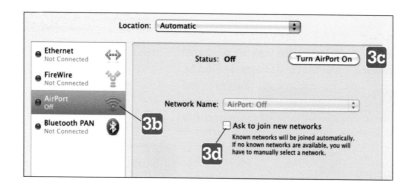

! **ALERT:** Some establishments *will* require you to buy a beer, get a library card or rent a room to gain access to the network, and in some places will even require a password to make sure you do. Most don't, though.

! **ALERT:** If you can't make changes to the existing settings, click the lock in the bottom left corner of the Network window. Input your administrator name and password as required.

Tip 5: Use Safari Reader

Sometimes, when you come across an article you want to read on the Internet, the elements included with the article are distracting. If you have a visual impairment or if you use VoiceOver when surfing the Web (and it tries to read these elements), keep an eye out for the Reader icon in Safari's Address bar. If you see it, you can click it to view the article with fewer distractions.

1 Visit www.wikipedia.com.

2 Browse the articles by clicking links on any page.

3 When you see Reader in the Address bar, click it.

4 Use the controls to zoom in or out as desired, to email the page or to print it, or to close the Reader window.

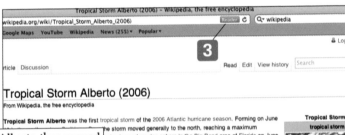

Big Bend area of Florida on June 13. Alberto then moved through eastern Georgia, North Carolina, and Virginia as a tropical depression before becoming extratropical on June 14.

Across the Western Caribbean, the storm produced heavy rainfall, causing some minor damage. In Florida, a moderate storm tide caused coastal damage and flooding, whi[...]nds produced several tornad[...]ctly responsible

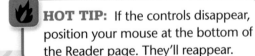

4

 HOT TIP: If the controls disappear, position your mouse at the bottom of the Reader page. They'll reappear.

HOT TIP: If you want to print an article you find on the web and Reader is an option, click it and print from the Reader. Many of the elements you won't want to print, such as the ads, will be removed.

? DID YOU KNOW?
You can click the X in the controls to close the Reader or simply click Reader again in the Address bar.

Tip 6: Download and install a program from the Internet

Although we suggest you stay away from most downloads, there are programs you'll need. For instance, you'll need to download Flash Player to watch certain web videos. Or you may want to purchase something from Apple such as an OS update, QuickTime Pro, or iWork. The download process is the same for all of them.

1 Locate something you want to download and click the Download link.

2 Click the Install option. You may see this option in more than one place.

3 When presented with the warning box, click Open to continue.

4 If applicable, perform any preinstallation tasks, such as agreeing to Terms of Service.

5 Click Install.

6 Type your password and click OK.

7 Wait while the program installs.

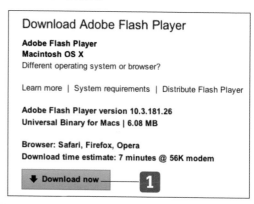

Download Adobe Flash Player

Adobe Flash Player
Macintosh OS X
Different operating system or browser?

Learn more | System requirements | Distribute Flash Player

Adobe Flash Player version 10.3.181.26
Universal Binary for Macs | 6.08 MB

Browser: Safari, Firefox, Opera
Download time estimate: 7 minutes @ 56K modem

⬇ Download now **1**

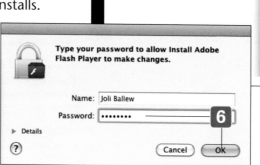

ALERT: It's often difficult to know whether a download is safe or not. The best way to find out is to read reviews and search the internet for user comments and complaints.

ALERT: You may be prompted to close related programs before installing a program. If so, click the title bar of the application to make it active, then from the Menu bar quit the application.

? DID YOU KNOW?
Downloading and installing an application are two separate things. Once a download is complete you must still perform the installation.

Tip 7: Manage junk email

Junk email is email you don't want from people you do not know. Email that Mail thinks is junk is shown in gold in your inbox. You'll want to train Mail so that it knows when an email is junk and when it isn't.

1 Click any email that Mail thinks is junk.

2 If it is not junk, click Not Junk. (You can also opt to load any images.)

3 Click any email that Mail thinks is not junk.

4 If it is junk, click Junk.

5 To configure junk email preferences:

 a. Click Mail>Preferences from the Menu bar.

 b. Click Junk Mail.

 c. Configure junk mail options as desired.

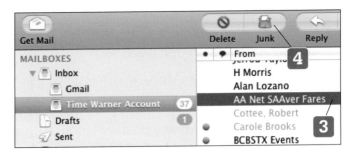

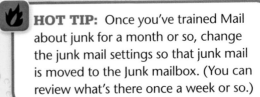

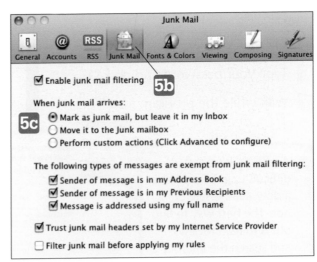

HOT TIP: Need to write yourself a quick note? In Mail, click Note and start typing!

HOT TIP: Once you've trained Mail about junk for a month or so, change the junk mail settings so that junk mail is moved to the Junk mailbox. (You can review what's there once a week or so.)

Tip 8: Listen to free iTunes U content

The iTunes Store offers a section called iTunes U. There you can access free lectures from colleges and universities all over the world. You browse the iTunes U store the same way you browse for other iTunes Store media; you listen to downloaded media in the same way, too.

1 In iTunes, click iTunes Store in the left pane.

2 Click iTunes U at the top of the iTunes window.

3 Browse what's offered.

4 When you find something you like, click Free.

5 When the download completes, locate the item in the iTunes U section of iTunes to play it.

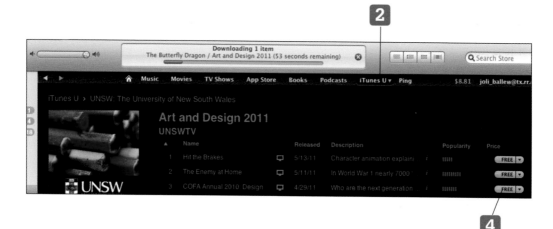

🔥 **HOT TIP:** Remember the Back button! It will take you to the previous page. If you ever get lost, though, just click iTunes U at the top of the iTunes window to start again.

❓ **DID YOU KNOW?**
While browsing iTunes U, you can choose a category that interests you, such as Fine Arts, Literature, or Social Science to narrow the results.

Tip 9: Back up with Time Machine

Time Machine is an application included with your Mac that lets you back up your data automatically. Time Machine keeps hourly backups for the past 24 hours, daily backups for the past month and weekly backups for the previous months until the disk you're backing up to is full. Then it writes over the oldest backups.

1 Open System Preferences>Time Machine.

2 Move the slider from Off to On.

3 Choose the external drive from the list of drives when prompted. (If you aren't prompted, click Select Disk.)

4 Click the disk and then click Use for Backup.

5 A backup will occur automatically.

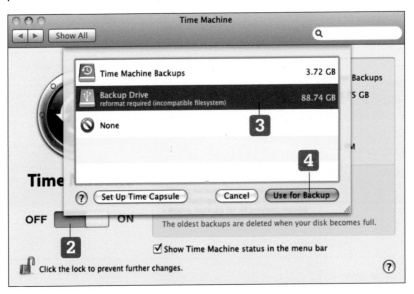

ALERT: You'll need an external backup device such as an external hard drive to get started with Time Machine. Ideally, it should be at least 160 GB.

ALERT: If you're prompted to erase what's currently on the drive, create a backup of it first on another computer if possible, or choose another backup device

Tip 10: Enable and use Zoom

Zoom lets you use a keyboard combination to enable Zoom and to zoom in and out. Once you get used to the commands, it's extremely easy (and convenient) to use this feature. Zoom lets you zoom in on anything, not just a webpage or other item.

1 Open System Preferences>Universal Access.

2 From the Seeing tab, note the keyboard commands and try them now.

3 Click Options.

4 Set Maximum and Minimum Zoom.

Zoom:
⦿ On ○ Off

Turn zoom on or off: ⌥⌘8
Zoom in: ⌥⌘=
Zoom out: ⌥⌘–

3 (Options...)

5 Review other settings and click Done.

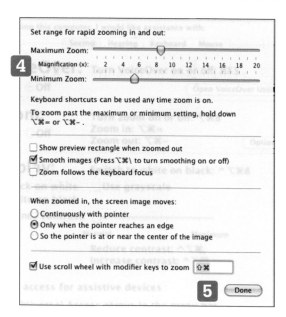

Set range for rapid zooming in and out.

Maximum Zoom:
Magnification (x): 2 4 6 8 10 12 14 16 18 20
Minimum Zoom:

Keyboard shortcuts can be used any time zoom is on.

To zoom past the maximum or minimum setting, hold down ⌥⌘= or ⌥⌘– .

☐ Show preview rectangle when zoomed out
☑ Smooth images (Press ⌥⌘\ to turn smoothing on or off)
☐ Zoom follows the keyboard focus

When zoomed in, the screen image moves:
○ Continuously with pointer
⦿ Only when the pointer reaches an edge
○ So the pointer is at or near the center of the image

☑ Use scroll wheel with modifier keys to zoom [⇧⌘]

5 (Done)

HOT TIP: Practise this several times now, write down the key combination and leave it by the keyboard. It's a very helpful thing to know and may let you forgo the reading glasses!

WHAT DOES THIS MEAN?

Zoom: With a Mac keyboard you turn on Zoom by holding down the Option and Command and 8 keys together; zoom in with Option and Command and = keys together; zoom out with Option and Command and – keys together. Press as many times as necessary to zoom in and out effectively.

Zoom: With a Windows keyboard you turn on Zoom by holding down the Alt and Windows and 8 keys together; zoom in with Alt and Windows and = keys together; zoom out with Alt and Windows and – keys together. Press as many times as necessary to zoom in and out effectively.

1 Get to know your Mac

Introduction

Even though there are various types of Mac computers, including the different types of MacBooks, the iMac, Mac mini and Mac Pro, they all run some version of the Mac OS X software. Your Mac might have Jaguar, Panther, Tiger, Leopard, Snow Leopard or Lion for an operating system (OS), for instance. Don't worry, though, we'll get you going with whatever type of Mac you have and whatever OS you have installed.

Thus, to keep it generic and applicable to all different types of OS, in this chapter you'll learn what's available on the screen, from the Dock and hidden away in the Dashboard, how to interact with your Mac using dialogue boxes and similar elements, and how to check for free software updates. These are features available on all Macs. Later in the book we may point out features specific to a particular OS, but don't worry, we'll let you know.

Explore the Menu bar

Your Mac has several items on its screen. There are two you want to become familiar with right away: the Menu bar and the Dock. The Menu bar runs across the top of the screen and changes depending on what's open on the Mac's Desktop.

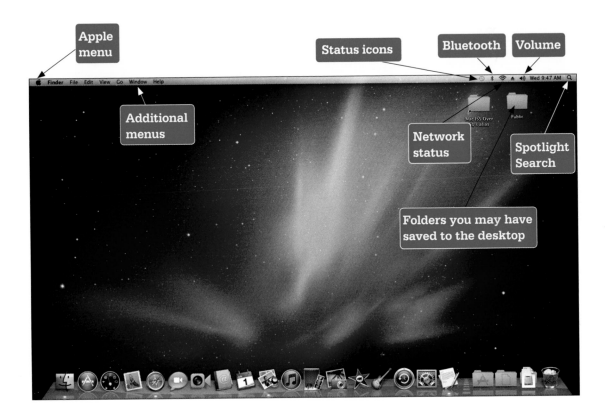

Apple menu

Status icons

Bluetooth

Volume

Additional menus

Network status

Spotlight Search

Folders you may have saved to the desktop

The Menu bar offers some things all the time:

● The Apple menu: you'll use this menu to change settings related to your Mac, such as updating its software or shutting down the computer.

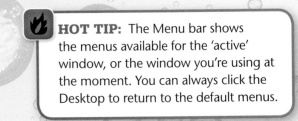

HOT TIP: The Menu bar shows the menus available for the 'active' window, or the window you're using at the moment. You can always click the Desktop to return to the default menus.

- Additional menus: when applications are open, you'll have access to their menus. When you open a new program like Safari, shown here, the items on the Menu bar will change.

- Status icons: You'll always have access to the Volume icon, the network status icon and the Spotlight Search icon, as well as the time, among other things.

WHAT DOES THIS MEAN?

'Desktop': What you see when there's nothing open on the screen. It's the large area with the starburst, shown above.

Explore the Dock

The Dock runs across the bottom of the screen and holds icons you can click to open their related program or window. Some show status icons, like the Mail icon below. (This means there are two unread email messages.) Open programs appear here, too, and have a graphic with them. Here, that graphic is a small, circular light that appears underneath, but what you see may differ.

1 Note the icons on the Dock. See whether any have status icons on them or graphics underneath.

2 Hover the mouse over any icon. Notice its name appear over the top of it.

3 Click any icon once to open the window or program.

4 Click the red X in any window to close it.

HOT TIP: If you had trouble reading what was shown in step 2 because the print was too small, enable magnification on the Dock, detailed in the next section.

HOT TIP: To add an item to the Dock, drag it to it. You can add programs, files, folders, websites and more.

DID YOU KNOW?
You can move the Dock's position from the System Preferences icon. You'll learn how to do that in the next section.

Magnify the Dock

Because you'll be using the Dock quite often, it's best to configure it so you can see it properly right from the start. This will help you better use your Mac and help you personalise it to suit your needs.

1. On the Dock, click the System Preferences icon.

2. From the System Preferences window, click Dock.

3. Move the size slider to Large.

4. Click Magnification and move to Max.

5. To reposition the Dock, select a new position on the screen. (We suggest you leave it at the bottom for now.)

6. Hover your mouse over any icon on the Dock to see the magnification feature.

HOT TIP: Before clicking Dock in step 2, note all of the other System Preferences options, including Appearance, Desktop & Screen Saver, and more. You'll explore some of these in Chapter 2. (If you missed it, click Show All.)

DID YOU KNOW?

When in System Preferences, and in a particular setting option (such as Dock in steps 3–5), you can click Show All to return to the main System Preferences screen.

Explore the Apple menu

The Apple menu is on the Menu bar, no matter what other menus are showing or what program or window is active. When you click the Apple icon, you have access to various computer options, including putting the computer to sleep, shown here.

The Apple menu options vary depending on what version of Mac OS X you're running. Here are a few you should become familiar with:

- About This Mac. Click to view information about your computer, including your Mac OS X version, type of processor and amount of memory.

- Software Update. Click to see whether any updates are available for your Mac.

- App Store. Click to access the App Store to obtain apps, games, business tools and more.

- System Preferences. Click to access the System Preferences window, introduced in the previous section.

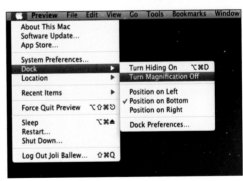

- Dock. Click to set Dock preferences quickly.

- Force Quit. Click to quit any program that is not responding or is frozen.

- Sleep, Restart or Shut Down. Use these options when you need to put the computer to sleep, restart it or shut it down.

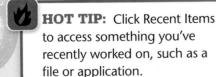

HOT TIP: Click Recent Items to access something you've recently worked on, such as a file or application.

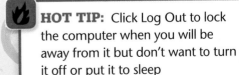

HOT TIP: Click Log Out to lock the computer when you will be away from it but don't want to turn it off or put it to sleep

Use the Finder

The Finder is the first icon on the Dock, to the far left. This opens the Finder window. Once open, you'll find various options, including the ability to navigate your entire hard drive. You'll use the Finder regularly to find files, open applications and search for images, movies and other data.

1 Click Finder on the Dock to open it.

2 In the left pane, click your user name.

3 Click any folder listed and then click subfolders, if they are available.

4 Click the four view options to see how the view changes.

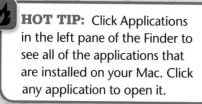

HOT TIP: Click Applications in the left pane of the Finder to see all of the applications that are installed on your Mac. Click any application to open it.

? DID YOU KNOW?
The Finder orders things hierarchically. When you click one item, most of the time a 'sub-item' opens.

5 Note the menu options on the Menu bar. You'll see File, Edit, View, Go, Window and Help. Click each to see what's available.

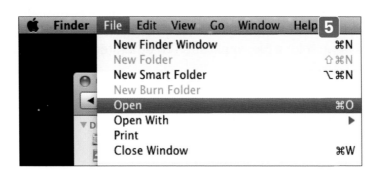

Search with Finder

Sometimes, browsing through the folders in the Finder can become onerous. An alternative to browsing is to search. The Finder window contains a Spotlight Search box that you can use to search for a file, application or other item by name.

1 Click the Finder icon on the Dock to open it.

2 Click inside the Spotlight Search window.

3 Type what you're looking for. (Note that you can change the view options to show thumbnails, as we did here, if you wish.)

4 Click any item to open it. If you open a folder, you will have to click again on the item to open.

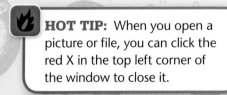
HOT TIP: When you open a picture or file, you can click the red X in the top left corner of the window to close it.

? DID YOU KNOW?
If you receive an error and are prompted to 'Fix Alias', do so. An alias is a shortcut, and often, shortcuts can become 'orphaned' and no longer be associated with a particular file.

Start an application

Applications are programs you use to perform tasks. You can use the TextEdit program to write a letter, iTunes to acquire and listen to music, and Safari to surf the Internet. To start an application, you simply click it.

1 On the Dock, open iCal.

2 Notice the Menu bar changes. You'll see iCal, File, Edit, Calendar, View, Window and Help.

3 Next, open the Finder.

4 In the Finder window, click Applications.

5 Now, double-click Calculator. (We've changed the view to thumbnails.) Note the Menu bar now.

> **?** **DID YOU KNOW?**
> You can open an application from the Dock if it's there; otherwise, use the Finder's Applications option.

> **HOT TIP:** When in the Finder and in Applications, consider thumbnail view, shown here. It may be easier on your over-50 eyes!

> **?** **DID YOU KNOW?**
> If you have an Apple mouse, you can use the little dot in the middle of that mouse to scroll through icons in windows that run more than the length of it.

Explore an application window

In the previous section you learned how to open an application in two ways, using the Dock and using the Finder. Once open, you know that the Menu bar changes. Whichever application is 'active', or in use, is the one the Menu bar reflects. You can use these tools to perform tasks with the open application.

1 Open TextEdit (and this is a different technique than detailed earlier):

   a. Click the Spotlight Search icon on the Menu bar – it's the magnifying glass.

   b. Type TextEdit.

   c. Click TextEdit in the results.

2 From the Menu bar, click Format, click Font and click Bigger. Note the keyboard combination (Command and +). You can use this key combination instead of the menu, if you like.

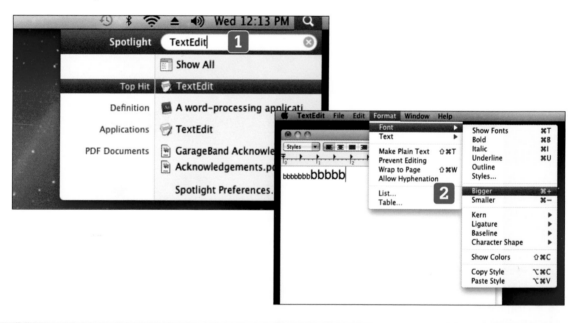

3 From the Menu menu, click File. Note the options to save or print the file. You'll learn more about this later in the book.

4 From the Edit menu, note the options to check spelling and grammar, among other things.

5 From the Help menu, note the option to search for help on a given topic by typing keywords.

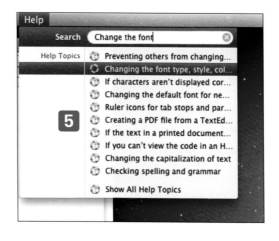

Help

| Search | Change the font ⊗ |

Help Topics

- 🔅 Preventing others from changing...
- 🔅 Changing the font type, style, col...
- 🔅 If characters aren't displayed cor...
- 🔅 Changing the default font for ne...
- 🔅 Ruler icons for tab stops and par...
- 🔅 Creating a PDF file from a TextEd...
- 🔅 If the text in a printed document...
- 🔅 If you can't view the code in an H...
- 🔅 Changing the capitalization of text
- 🔅 Checking spelling and grammar

- 🔅 Show All Help Topics

HOT TIP: You can have lots of windows and applications open at the same time. However, if you have too many open at once, your computer may perform more slowly than you're used to.

Switch between applications with Exposé

When you have multiple applications and windows open, you may find it difficult to move from one to the other. Clicking the icon in the Dock can be onerous, as can clicking the window itself to make it active. Exposé is a feature that lets you move easily among your open apps.

1 From the Dock, click System Preferences.

2 Under Personal, click Exposé & Spaces.

3 Make a note of how Exposé should be used. Here, you can open all windows by pressing F9 on the keyboard. You can show the Application windows by pressing F10. And you can show the Desktop by pressing F11.

4 If applicable, open other applications and windows. Then press F9 (or whatever key is set to open 'all windows') to use Exposé.

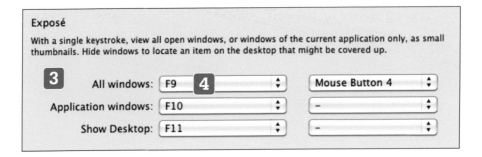

Exposé

With a single keystroke, view all open windows, or windows of the current application only, as small thumbnails. Hide windows to locate an item on the desktop that might be covered up.

3 All windows:	F9 **4**	Mouse Button 4
Application windows:	F10	–
Show Desktop:	F11	–

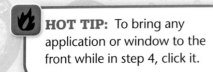 **HOT TIP:** To bring any application or window to the front while in step 4, click it.

 **DID YOU KNOW?**

If F9 is a difficult key for you to press because it is small, in step 3 you can change it to a key that's larger. Try right Shift if this is the case. (Then, pressing the right Shift key will invoke Exposé.)

5 Click Esc on the keyboard, press the F9 key, or use the mouse to click anywhere on the Desktop to return to the previous view.

ALERT: The way Exposé works differs for the various Mac OS editions. Thus it's important to review the settings in System Preferences first.

Explore the Dashboard

The Dashboard is a hidden feature that offers 'widgets' you can use to quickly get information and perform common tasks. Default widgets include a calculator, a weather app, a calendar app and a clock. As with Exposé, you can invoke the Dashboard with a keystroke (or a mouse click).

1 Press the F12 key on the keyboard or click the Dashboard icon on the Dock.

2 Notice the widgets that appear on the Desktop. Using the mouse, click a few numbers on the Calculator.

3 Click the + sign in the bottom left corner. Click any widget to add it to the Dashboard.

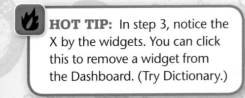

HOT TIP: In step 3, notice the X by the widgets. You can click this to remove a widget from the Dashboard. (Try Dictionary.)

4 Click the + sign again to close the add widget options.

5 Click the title bar of any widget and drag it to place it somewhere else on the screen.

6 Click an empty area of the Desktop or press F12 to close the widget screen.

 HOT TIP: In the System Preferences app, under Exposé & Spaces, you can change the keystroke required to invoke Dashboard and choose any other Function key. If the Function keys are difficult for you to access, you can use a mouse button instead.

 HOT TIP: Some widgets, such as the Calculator widget, are interactive and accept user input. Others offer a small i in the bottom right corner that enable you to personalise them.

Use a dialogue box, sheet or window

Often, and under various circumstances, you'll be prompted to make a choice, input a password or otherwise interact with a system feature, such as a dialogue box, sheet or window. Here, an iTunes prompt is shown, requiring user input to complete a purchase.

Beyond inputting a password, you will be prompted, on occasion, to interact with an item on the screen to, among other things:

- Configure settings.

- Set up devices.

- Make a selection.

- Move a slider.

- Name a file.

- Choose a location to save a file.

- Name a folder.

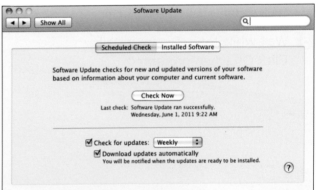

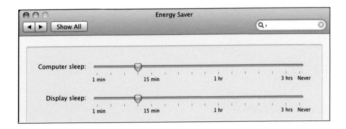

 ALERT: The prompt to input your password before performing system-wide changes or making purchases is a security feature. It's there to protect you, not annoy you!

? DID YOU KNOW?
Unlike Windows computers, you generally don't have to click Save or Apply when making configuration changes to your Mac

Get software updates

It doesn't matter how old or how new your Mac is, there may be software updates available. It's good to check for updates every couple of months, just to make sure you haven't missed any.

1 From the Menu bar that runs across the top of the screen, click the Apple menu icon.

2 Click Software Update.

3 If an update is available, click Show Details. (If no updates are available, click Quit.)

4 Select the items to install and click Install ___ Item(s).

5 Wait while the software installs. Click OK when prompted.

 DID YOU KNOW?
You can check for updates to other software from inside the application. For instance, in iTunes, click the iTunes menu and click Check for Updates.

HOT TIP: A couple of times a year, check for updates for third-party applications you've installed.

ALERT: Security updates help keep your Mac safe and secure. You should install them.

Get iTunes, iPod, iPad and iPhone updates

To check for updates to iTunes, open iTunes and from the Menu bar, click iTunes, then click Check for Updates. Install the updates as prompted. If you use i-devices with iTunes on your Mac, you should check for updates for them, too.

1 If applicable, connect your i-device to your Mac.

2 In iTunes, click the device in the left pane.

3 From the Summary tab, click Update or Check for Updates.

4 Click Update and work through the resulting dialogue boxes.

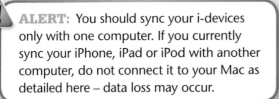

ALERT: You should sync your i-devices only with one computer. If you currently sync your iPhone, iPad or iPod with another computer, do not connect it to your Mac as detailed here – data loss may occur.

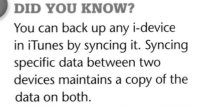

DID YOU KNOW?

You can back up any i-device in iTunes by syncing it. Syncing specific data between two devices maintains a copy of the data on both.

5 Wait while the process completes.

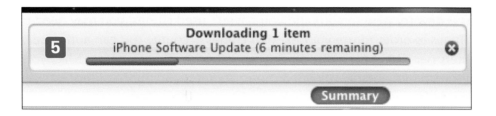

Authorise iTunes

If your Mac is new (or new to you) and you haven't used iTunes, you may need to authorise iTunes in order to use your existing iTunes account. You can authorise up to five computers per iTunes account. When you authorise iTunes on your Mac, you can access your purchased and downloaded music, movies, audiobooks, podcasts, apps and the like from it.

1 Open iTunes. Make sure it's active and that iTunes is showing on the Menu bar.

2 From the Store menu, click Authorize This Computer.

3 Type your iTunes account name and password.

4 Click Authorize.

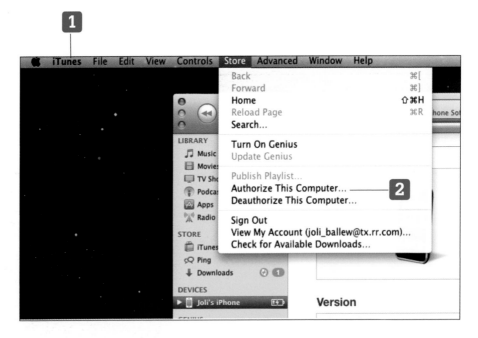

ALERT: Always deauthorise iTunes before handing a Mac down to your kids, donating it to a church or selling it. (Ultimately, you should restore it to factory settings.)

? DID YOU KNOW?

You may have authorised other items in iTunes. For instance, if you use Audible to acquire audiobooks, from the Advanced menu, you'll have options to authorise or deauthorise your Audible account.

Sleep, Restart, Shut Down and Log Out of your Mac

When you don't need to use your Mac you have three choices: Log Off, Sleep and Shut Down. (You could also do nothing.) When you have a problem with your Mac, you can restart it, too. All of these choices are available from the Apple menu.

● Sleep: Select when you want the computer to rest but not be shut down. When you bring the computer out of sleep you are not prompted to input a password (although you can change this behaviour in System Preferences > Security (General tab)).

● Restart: Select when prompted or when the computer isn't responding as expected.

● Shut Down: Select when you won't be using your Mac for more than two days to save electricity or any time to preserve battery life on a laptop.

● Log Out: Select to log off of your account and lock the computer screen.

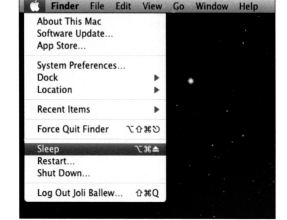

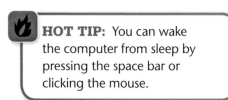

HOT TIP: You can wake the computer from sleep by pressing the space bar or clicking the mouse.

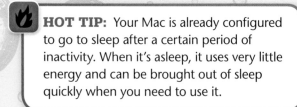

HOT TIP: Your Mac is already configured to go to sleep after a certain period of inactivity. When it's asleep, it uses very little energy and can be brought out of sleep quickly when you need to use it.

DID YOU KNOW?
You can change when the computer sleeps from the System Preferences app, under Energy Saver.

Add icons to the Dock

You may have removed icons in the previous section you want back, or you may want to add icons for applications you use often that aren't there by default. In either case, you'll want to add icons to the Dock.

1 Open Finder from the Dock and click Applications. Alternatively, you can open Applications directly from the Dock.

2 Locate the icon you want to add to the Dock.

3 Drag it to the Dock and drop it there.

4 To move the icon to a new place on the Dock, drag it there.

HOT TIP: You can configure the Dock to hide when you aren't using it and show when you move your mouse to the default Dock area. You do this from System Preferences>Dock.

ALERT: The Dock you see here and the Dock you see on your computer may no longer look the same. Remember, you can access any icon you've removed from the Applications window, as detailed above.

Configure Dashboard icons

You learned a little about the Dashboard in Chapter 1. You enable the Dashboard from its associated icon on the Dock. The widgets that appear on the Dashboard can be customised to meet your needs, and you can add and remove Dashboard widgets easily.

1 Click the Dashboard icon on the Dock. If you have removed it, open it from the Finder or the Applications window.

2 Hover the mouse over each icon. If you see a small i, click it to configure the item. (Many items won't have configuration options.)

3 Configure the widget as desired. Click Done if applicable.

4 To delete a widget, click the + sign near the Dock.

5 Click any X to remove the widget. Likewise, click any widget to add it.

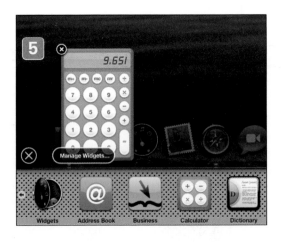

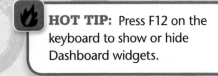

HOT TIP: Press F12 on the keyboard to show or hide Dashboard widgets.

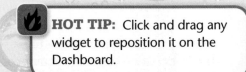

HOT TIP: Click and drag any widget to reposition it on the Dashboard.

Add and rearrange Desktop icons

You can save files to the Desktop, create aliases (shortcuts) for items you access often, and even drag folders there to make them accessible from the Desktop. As time goes on, you may find your Desktop has too many items on it, or that you want to rearrange them.

1 To move any item on the Desktop from one area to another, drag it there.

2 To remove any item from the Desktop, drag it to the Trash can on the Dock.

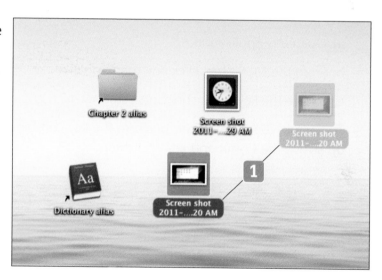

DID YOU KNOW?

You can create an alias for any application and have access to it on the Desktop. (An alias for the Dictionary application is shown in the figure here.) To do this, in Finder, click Applications, select the application, and then from the File menu, select Make Alias. You can then drag the alias to the Desktop.

HOT TIP: You can restore anything from the Trash. Just click Trash on the Dock and drag the item from the Trash to the Desktop.

ALERT: You can drag aliases to the Trash can with no loss of data. However, if you drag items to the Trash can that contain real data, the actual data will be deleted.

Use and configure keyboard shortcuts

If you have trouble using a mouse or just prefer to use the keyboard to perform tasks, you'll enjoy using and creating keyboard shortcuts. Almost every task you can imagine already has a shortcut associated with it and/or can be configured.

1 To view keyboard shortcuts already in place:

   a. Open any application.

   b. From the Menu bar, click any menu option.

   c. Notice the keyboard shortcuts listed by each entry.

2 To use a keyboard shortcut, perform the key combination offered. Here, that's the up arrow, the Command key and the A.

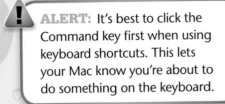

ALERT: It's best to click the Command key first when using keyboard shortcuts. This lets your Mac know you're about to do something on the keyboard.

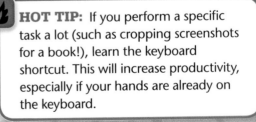

HOT TIP: If you perform a specific task a lot (such as cropping screenshots for a book!), learn the keyboard shortcut. This will increase productivity, especially if your hands are already on the keyboard.

3 To assign a keyboard shortcut:

a. Click System Preferences, then click Keyboard.

b. Click the Keyboard Shortcuts tab.

c. Click the + sign.

d. Click in the Application window and select the application for which to create a shortcut.

e. Type a menu title.

f. Perform the keyboard shortcut to use.

g. Click Add.

DID YOU KNOW?

You can view keyboard shortcuts already in place in System Preferences>Keyboard>Keyboard Shortcuts. In the left pane, select the area to explore, and in the right pane, review the shortcuts already configured.

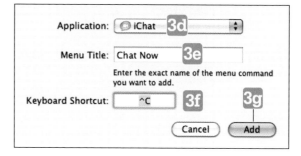

HOT TIP: When creating a shortcut, try to make it easy to remember. For instance, use Control + C to open iChat, or Control + P to open iPhoto.

HOT TIP: You can always restore the defaults for keyboard shortcuts from the Keyboard Shortcuts window in step 3b here.

Customise how the mouse works

Sometimes a mouse is difficult to use, especially if it's extremely small or if your hands are exceptionally large. Bigger problems exist when your hands are arthritic or if they shake or tremble. When these issues occur, you can make configuration changes in System Preferences to make the mouse easier to handle.

1 Click System Preferences.

2 Click Mouse.

3 If your hands are shaky, consider slowing down the tracking speed.

4 If you have trouble double-clicking, consider slowing down the double-click speed.

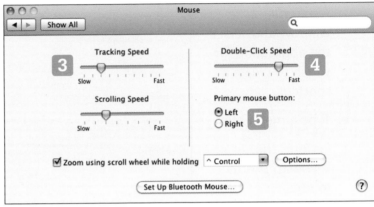

5 If you want to use the mouse with your left hand instead of your right, change the primary mouse button.

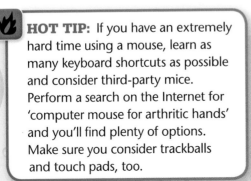

HOT TIP: Tired of being tethered to your computer via your mouse? Purchase and configure a Bluetooth or wireless mouse.

HOT TIP: If you have an extremely hard time using a mouse, learn as many keyboard shortcuts as possible and consider third-party mice. Perform a search on the Internet for 'computer mouse for arthritic hands' and you'll find plenty of options. Make sure you consider trackballs and touch pads, too.

? DID YOU KNOW?
If you have connected a trackpad or have a laptop with one, click Trackpad in System Preferences to configure it or change the default settings.

WHAT DOES THIS MEAN?

Trackpad: A flat surface, included with laptops but now sold separately for desktop computers, that is used in place of a mouse.

Change power options

Your computer goes to sleep after a specific period of time. Likewise, the display is darkened. This saves power and energy, and in the case of a laptop, lengthens battery life. You may find that your computer goes to sleep too quickly, or not quickly enough. You can change how and when in the Energy Saver options in System Preferences.

1 Click System Preferences and click Energy Saver.

2 Move the sliders for Computer sleep and Display sleep to the desired time frame.

3 Review the other options and make changes as desired.

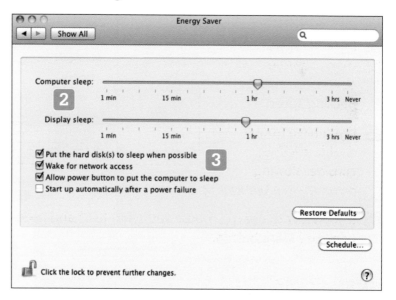

DID YOU KNOW?

Your Mac will not restart by default after a power failure. If it should, configure it so that it will. This is important if your Mac is configured to perform tasks at a specific time each day and needs to be on to get the job done.

HOT TIP: When using a laptop from battery power, configure the computer and display to go to sleep quickly, perhaps after 5 minutes of inactivity, to conserve battery life.

HOT TIP: Click Schedule to configure exact days and times the computer should start up or sleep.

Make aliases for the Desktop

An alias, in Mac-speak, is a shortcut to something. You can create aliases for folders and applications (among other things) and place those aliases on the Desktop to make them easier to open. For instance, you can create an alias for the Movies folder, so you can access it from the Desktop instead of having to open the Finder to get to it.

1 Open Finder from the Dock.

2 Locate any item you'd like to create an alias for and click it once.

3 On the keyboard, click Command + L. (Alternatively, you could click the File menu and click Make Alias.)

4 Drag the alias to the Desktop.

HOT TIP: You can drag any alias to the Dock and drop it there if you need an alias but don't want to clutter up your Desktop with icons.

DID YOU KNOW?
You can create aliases for applications, documents, PDF files, images and folders, among other things.

ALERT: You can drag any alias to the Trash without fear of losing any data. Aliases are simply shortcuts to data stored elsewhere and do not, in themselves, hold any actual data.

Explore sounds and configure sound devices

You can adjust the sound from the Menu bar using the available Volume icon. Sometimes you need to change more than just the volume, though. You may want to turn off sounds for specific events, configure external speakers, or change the input volume for a microphone or webcam, among other things.

1 Open System Preferences from the Dock.

2 Click Sounds.

3 To change the volume of sounds associated with alerts, from the Sound Effects tab, move the slider for Alert volume to the left or right.

4 To change, configure or select the output device to use, click the Output tab and make the appropriate choices.

5 To change, configure or select an input device to use, click the Input tab and make the appropriate choices.

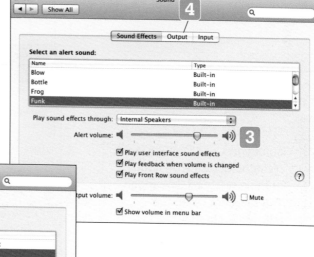

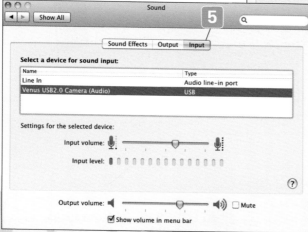

HOT TIP: To remove the Volume icon from the Menu bar, deselect Show volume in Menu bar.

HOT TIP: If you have more than one output device, select the one to use from Sound Effects, next to Play sound effects through.

Install hardware

Most of the time, all you have to do to install Mac-compatible hardware is connect it, plug it in and turn it on. You may have to insert a CD or DVD that contains additional software and perform an installation, but often that's not the case.

1 Read any directions that come with the hardware.

2 If the directions instruct you to install software from a CD, do so.

3 Plug the device into a wall outlet if applicable.

4 Plug the device into the appropriate port on the Mac.

5 Turn the device on.

6 If applicable, perform any additional steps as prompted.

7 Locate the device on your Mac. You'll find i-devices in iTunes, shown here.

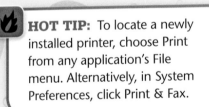

? DID YOU KNOW?
Sometimes you'll connect something, turn it on and nothing will seem to happen. This does not mean the hardware didn't install. In fact, the hardware is more than likely ready to use!

HOT TIP: To locate a newly installed printer, choose Print from any application's File menu. Alternatively, in System Preferences, click Print & Fax.

HOT TIP: Webcams and other input devices can be found in System Preferences, under Sound>Input.

Install a Bluetooth device

Bluetooth devices are those devices that can connect to your Mac wirelessly, using Bluetooth technology. You may want to purchase a Bluetooth mouse, or you may already have other Bluetooth devices available. You have to set up Bluetooth devices manually.

1 Open System Preferences and click Bluetooth.

2 Verify that On and Discoverable are ticked, and then click Set Up New Device.

3 Select the device in the Bluetooth Setup Assistant window and click Continue.

4 Wait while the device is 'paired' or matched to your device.

5 Once paired, click Pair on the device to pair it.

ALERT: If a device won't pair, read the error messages carefully. Often, there's a problem with the configuration of the device itself and rarely a problem with your Mac's ability to find or connect to it.

3 Work with windows, files and folders

Introduction

When you open the Finder, iTunes or Safari (among other items), they open in a container called a window. That window may offer view options, access to any files and folders stored there, and/or the ability to use features available in it. As an example, the iTunes window offers tools for managing and playing media, while the Finder window offers tools for navigating the data and applications on the hard drive. Each window is different. As you'll learn here, understanding these three areas and what each offers (windows, files and folders) is the secret to understanding how to navigate, organise and use your Mac effectively.

Locate default data folders using the Finder

The Finder is available from the Dock – it's the icon on the far left. The Finder is what you use to navigate your Mac and to find the data and applications stored on it. The Finder is organised like a filing cabinet and already includes some folders to help you get started, such as Documents, Movies, Music, Pictures and others.

1 Open the Finder from the Dock.

2 In the sidebar (the left pane), select your user name. Here, that's joli_ballew.

3 Open any folder. This may require a single click or double click, depending on your mouse and its configuration.

4 Locate the Back button and click it to return to the previous window screen.

5 Continue opening folders and clicking the Back button until you are comfortable with what's in each folder.

HOT TIP: You may find that a folder, perhaps Pictures, already has subfolders and data, while others are empty.

ALERT: With some mice you must double-click to open a folder, with others a single-click will do.

DID YOU KNOW?
Instead of clicking the Back button you can click your user name under Places to return to the default Finder window.

Open a file from the Finder

You'll use the Finder to locate data. You can double-click any file to open it. Which window opens after you do this depends on the type of data you've opted to open. For instance, a picture will probably open in the Preview application, while a song will more likely open in iTunes.

1 Open the Finder and click your user name in the Sidebar.

2 Browse the default folders and any subfolders, and double-click a song, music video, movie, or picture to open.

 ALERT: On this page we've browsed to a song; however, on the next page we'll browse to and open a photo.

 ALERT: You will have to open multiple subfolders to get to music you've obtained from iTunes. You'll have to open Finder>Music>iTunes>iTunes Media>Music, then open the folder that contains the song to play. Finally, you can click the song to play it. It's much easier to open iTunes first and locate the music from inside the iTunes window.

3 Note the name of the application used to open the file on the Menu bar.

4 Note the name of the file.

5 Note any menu options or other features.

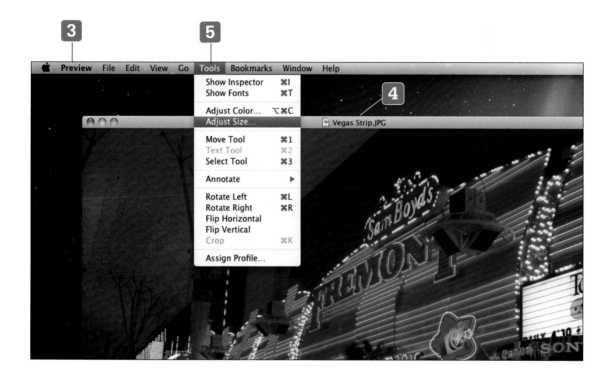

! ALERT: The Menu bar offers options for saving files, using tools, checking spelling and other application-specific features. However, the Menu bar isn't *in the window*, it's outside it.

Change the view in the Finder

You may have noticed in the first image in this chapter that the folders in our Finder window are much larger than yours. We made those folders appear larger using the zoom slider at the bottom of the Finder window. If your over-50 eyes are struggling to make out what's on the screen, you may want to make this change as well.

1 Open Finder and click your user name in the sidebar.

2 Verify that thumbnail view is selected.

3 Locate the slider in the bottom right corner and slide it towards the right.

4 If you're still having trouble making out what's on the screen, click the Quick Look icon.

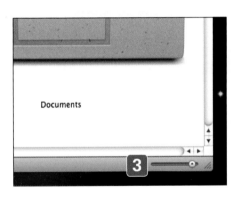

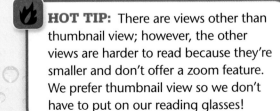

? DID YOU KNOW?

Ctrl + click (or right-click if applicable) to access the contextual menu for any folder. There you can make an alias for the folder, duplicate the folder, and more.

HOT TIP: There are views other than thumbnail view; however, the other views are harder to read because they're smaller and don't offer a zoom feature. We prefer thumbnail view so we don't have to put on our reading glasses!

Understand your Mac's folder hierarchy

You probably have a good idea, now that the default folders hold data, that those folders can have subfolders, and that any subfolders may have subfolders of their own. This is how the Mac organises data: it's hierarchical. To see the bigger picture, though, you have to dive into the actual hard drive, available from the Finder. This works only on Snow Leopard or earlier; it does not work this way on Lion.

1 Open the Finder and from the sidebar select Macintosh HD.

2 Note the folders: Applications, Library, System, User Guides And Information, and Users.

3 Open Applications to see what's there, then click the Back button.

4 Open Users to see what's there and explore subfolders as desired. Click Macintosh HD to return to the main HD screen.

5 Open User Guides And Information, and click Back when you're ready.

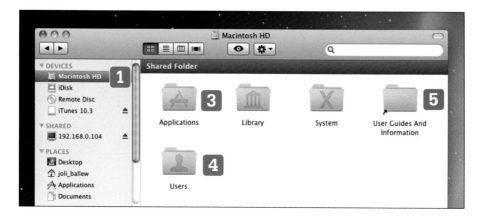

ALERT: Library and System are folders used by the Mac – there's no reason for you to go mucking about in there!

HOT TIP: Most users don't bother with the Macintosh HD option; instead they simply navigate their data using their user name under Places.

Create and name a folder or subfolder

As time passes, you'll eventually create or acquire so much data that it will become hard to manage. When this happens, you'll need to create your own folders and subfolders to organise it. This is useful with pictures and documents.

1 Open Finder and in the sidebar click Documents.

2 In the right pane, right-click or Ctrl + click to open the contextual menu. Click New Folder.

3 Type the name for the folder.

4 Press Enter on the keyboard.

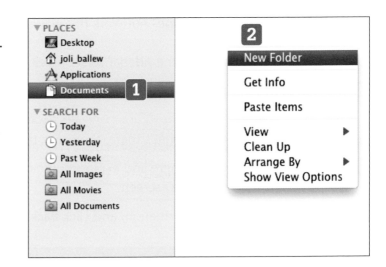

HOT TIP: To rename the folder once you've named it (or if you could not type a name in step 3), click the folder once to select it, press Enter on the keyboard, then type the name. Press Enter again to apply.

HOT TIP: Create subfolders in the Documents folder to hold like data, for instance Taxes, Classes, Projects, Legal, etc. Create subfolders in the Pictures folder named, perhaps, Grandkids, Kids, Weddings, Graduations, Hobbies, Holidays, etc.

DID YOU KNOW?

When you click Documents in the Sidebar of the Finder, you'll see the same thing as when you click your user name and then Documents from there.

Move a folder to the Finder's sidebar

Sometimes a folder won't be suitable for an existing subfolder such as Documents or Pictures, so a folder needs to be created to hold mixed data. For instance, you may create a folder called Travel and fill it with travel plans, ideas, documents, pictures from previous holidays and various informational documents. In these cases, you may want to create a folder and place it on the sidebar.

1 In the Finder, in Documents, create a folder. Name it appropriately.

2 Drag the new folder to the sidebar.

3 Be careful to drag it to an area in between existing folders and not on top of a folder.

4 Drop the new folder when you see the blue line, shown here.

5 Click the new folder in the sidebar to access it.

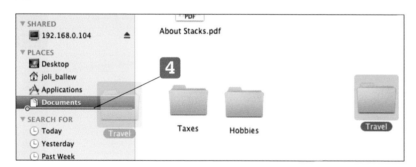

? DID YOU KNOW?
Removing a folder from the Sidebar that you've placed there will not result in any loss of data.

? DID YOU KNOW?
The folder will remain in the Documents folder but will appear on the sidebar. You can access it from either place.

🔥 HOT TIP: If you decide later you don't want the folder on the sidebar, Ctrl + click (or right-click it) and choose Remove from Sidebar.

Save data to a folder

You need to save data to the proper folders as you create it. You should save text documents to the Documents folder, for instance, and images to the applicable Pictures subfolder. You do this from the Save As dialogue box when you create data. In this exercise you'll create a short text document and save it to the Documents folder.

1 Open the Finder, click Applications in the Sidebar and click TextEdit. (Alternatively, click TextEdit on the Dock if it's there.)

2 Type a few words.

3 On the Menu bar, click File and click Save As.

4 Name the file.

5 Click the arrow next to Where to see some of the places you can save the file. Click Documents, the default.

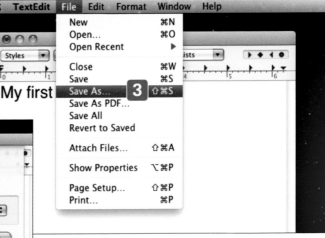

? DID YOU KNOW?
You can press the Ctrl key and the + key to increase the font quickly in TextEdit.

HOT TIP: When naming files, choose a name that will allow you to easily remember what it is, even if you look at it a year from now.

6 Click the arrow next to File Format to see the format options. Click Rich Text Format, the default.

7 Click Save.

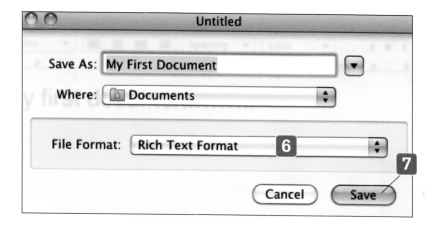

? **DID YOU KNOW?**

If you don't see where you want to save a file from the drop-down list, click the down arrow by the Save As window. This will expand the dialogue box and enable you to choose from additional options.

HOT TIP: Once you've saved a document to a specific place using the Save As command, all you have to do is use the key combination Command + S to save any future changes to the file. You can also access the Save command from the File menu.

HOT TIP: If you know you'll be sending the file to someone who uses Microsoft Word, save it in that format.

Move a folder

If you create a folder and decide later it should be somewhere else, you can move it. Moving isn't an option from any contextual menu though, and with folders there's no option to 'Cut' either. Thus, it's good to know a little trick for moving folders.

1 From the Finder, locate the folder to move.

2 Drag the folder to the Desktop.

3 From the Finder, locate the area where the moved folder should belong.

4 Drag the folder there.

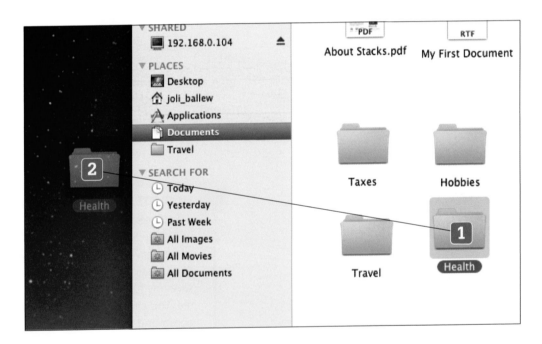

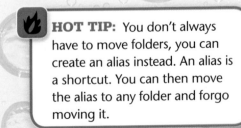

ALERT: This technique works only if you're moving a folder from one area of your Mac's hard drive to another area on your Mac's hard drive. If you drag from your Mac's hard drive to an external hard drive, the folder will be copied, not moved.

HOT TIP: You don't always have to move folders, you can create an alias instead. An alias is a shortcut. You can then move the alias to any folder and forgo moving it.

Rename, copy or delete a folder

On a Mac there are often multiple ways to perform a task. You can use a mouse click, a key combination, and often you can drag and drop. You can perform tasks from contextual menus, too, accessible from Ctrl + click or a right-click. So what we introduce here and elsewhere in this book is certainly not the only way to do something!

- To rename a folder: Click the folder once to select it. Press Enter on the keyboard. Type a new name. Press Enter again.

- To copy a folder: Ctrl + click or right-click and select Copy. (You can now repeat to paste the copied folder wherever you like.)

- Delete a folder: Drag the folder to the Trash icon on the Dock.

Favorite Activities

 Health

 Health

HOT TIP: Make sure you name folders so that you can tell what's in them without having to open them.

DID YOU KNOW?
You can restore items from the Trash provided you've yet to 'empty' the Trash. Just click the Trash icon and drag the items out, perhaps to the Desktop.

Copy or move a file

As you know, Copy is an option from most contextual menus. Move is not. You'll copy and move files the same way you copy and move folders, though. Remember, copying creates a duplicate, something you probably don't want, while moving actually moves the file to a new place.

- To copy a file: Ctrl + click or right-click and select Copy. Repeat the process to paste. Note you can also select Duplicate and then drag the duplicate file to the desired location.

- To move a file: Drag the file to the Desktop, then drag it to the appropriate area using the Finder.

🔥 HOT TIP: If you need access to a file in more than one place on your hard drive, say from the Travel folder, the Health folder and the Taxes folder, create an alias for it.

❓ DID YOU KNOW?
You can drag a file (or a folder) on top of another folder to move it there.

Rename or delete a file

You can rename a file and delete a file using the same techniques you learned earlier to rename and delete folders. For some variety, here are two additional techniques to try.

- To rename a file: Click Ctrl + click or right-click and choose Get Info. Under Name & Extension, type a new name.

- To delete a file: Ctrl + click or right-click, and from the contextual menu that appears, click Move to Trash.

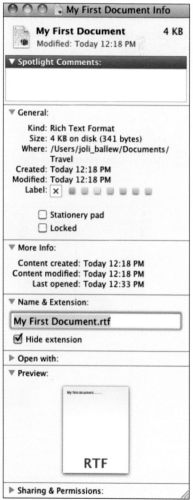

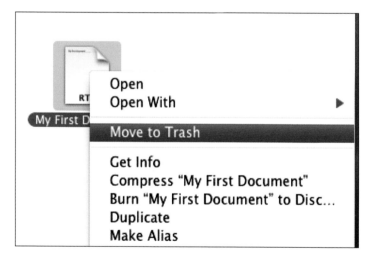

HOT TIP: Make sure you keep all documents in the Documents folder, all pictures in the Pictures folder, and so on.

DID YOU KNOW?
From the Get Info dialogue box you can 'label' the document with a specific colour. You might want to label anything that has to do with gardening green, travel blue, and taxes black!

Compress a file or folder

When you compress something you make it smaller. You can compress files and folders to make them take up less space on your hard drive, although this is generally done only for files that you plan to store long term and access rarely. Compression is more often applied to data prior to sending it in an email. Doing so helps the data get to the recipient faster than if it were not compressed.

1 Locate the data to compress.

2 Ctrl + click or right-click and choose Compress <name>.

3 If desired, drag the original file to the Trash.

4 When you need the data again, double-click the compressed file to open it.

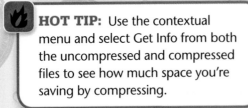 **HOT TIP:** Use the contextual menu and select Get Info from both the uncompressed and compressed files to see how much space you're saving by compressing.

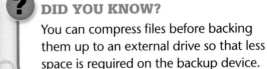 **DID YOU KNOW?**
You can compress files before backing them up to an external drive so that less space is required on the backup device.

Minimise, maximise, restore and close windows

When working with multiple open windows, you may want to move some from the screen by minimising them. Minimising causes the window to be reduced to an icon on the Dock. You can restore the window by clicking it. You can also close windows, quit applications and make the window larger or smaller to have more room on the Desktop for other items. To understand how these options work, it's best to apply them.

1 Open the TextEdit application.

2 Click the middle button with the – on it to minimise the application to the Dock.

3 Click its icon in the Dock to restore it to the Desktop.

4 Click the green + sign to get TextEdit to fill the entire screen. Click it again to restore it to its previous size.

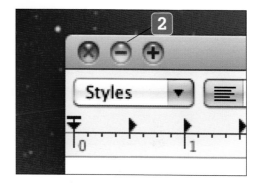

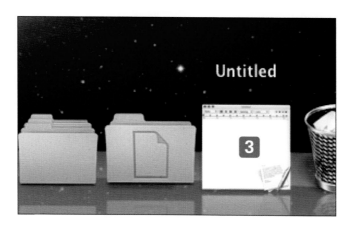

 HOT TIP: One way to locate TextEdit is to type Text in the Spotlight Search window on the far right side of the Menu bar.

DID YOU KNOW?
When you click the red X to 'close' a window it may still be active. You can tell from the Dock – if there's a white circle under it, it's still open and active.

5 Click the red X to minimise TextEdit to the Dock. Click the TextEdit icon on the Dock to restore it.

6 To quit an application, choose the application name from the Menu bar and opt to Quit the application.

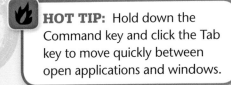

HOT TIP: Hold down the Command key and click the Tab key to move quickly between open applications and windows.

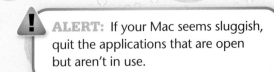

ALERT: If your Mac seems sluggish, quit the applications that are open but aren't in use.

4 Explore applications

Introduction

Lots of applications come preinstalled on your Mac. The applications you have access to let you perform tasks, play games, obtain media, send email and surf the Web, among other things. You can install your own applications, too; you may have opted to purchase and install iWork, for instance, or have software that came with a printer or scanner. You've probably already used a few applications, perhaps Safari to surf the Web, among others.

In this chapter you'll learn how to access, open and use some of the applications that come with your Mac. The first thing you'll learn to do is write a letter. If you have a printer, you can even print it out. With that out of the way, you'll find that using other applications will come naturally, and you'll get to explore your Mac in the process!

View all applications

Although you can access the applications on your Mac in various ways, the most straightforward is detailed here. You'll find you have lots of applications already installed on your Mac, and you'll have access to the Utilities folder with even more items to explore.

1 Open the Finder.

2 Under Places, click Applications.

3 Maximise the window and/or use the scroll bars as necessary to view the applications.

4 If your Applications window shows items in a list with small type, click the thumbnails view icon.

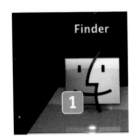

Finder

> **ALERT:** Many applications require you to be connected to the Internet. Refer to Chapter 5 to learn how to connect to a network or hotspot.

> **ALERT:** Your Finder window or Applications folder may not look exactly like the one shown here.

> **HOT TIP:** Use the slider in the bottom right corner of the window to enlarge the size of the icons when in thumbnail view (shown here).

Write and print a letter with TextEdit

TextEdit is an application that lets you write letters, to-do lists and similar documents. It does not have all of the features of a fully fledged word-processing program (such as Microsoft Word or Apple's Pages), but it may be all you need if you just want to type simple letters and notes.

1 In the Finder's Application window, open TextEdit.

2 Press the Command key and the + key multiple times to increase the font size.

3 Type your letter.

4 Click the File menu and click Print.

5 Set the print preferences as desired.

6 Click Print.

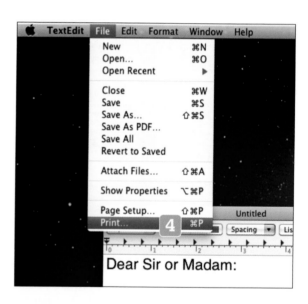

? DID YOU KNOW?
You can click File and then Page Setup between steps 3 and 4 and configure the page orientation, choose a paper size and more, all prior to printing.

! ALERT: The Command key on a Windows keyboard is the Windows key.

HOT TIP: If you don't see your printer listed, make sure it's connected, turned on and installed.

Look up a word using Dictionary

The Dictionary application lets you look up the definitions of words, but there's more to it than that. It is also a thesaurus and offers access to the Wikipedia and Apple websites, right from the interface.

1 From the Finder, open Dictionary.

2 Click the larger A a few times to increase the font size.

3 In the Spotlight Search window, type any word.

4 Select the desired entry.

5 Click Thesaurus, click Apple, then click Wikipedia to view their results.

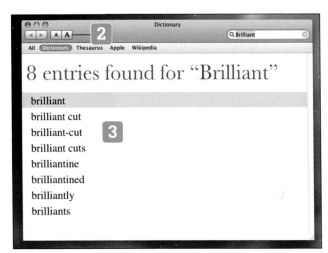

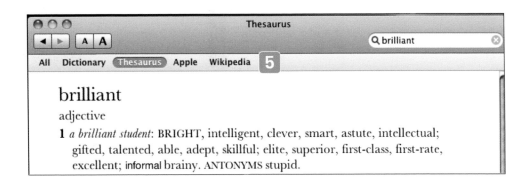

 ALERT: You won't always find entries under every option (in step 4).

 HOT TIP: Use the font buttons to increase and decrease the font size as needed.

Make a note with Stickies

As you get older, you may find yourself writing more and more notes about things you need to do, pick up or purchase. These notes can be misplaced easily, though. Stickies solves that problem by letting you make notes right on your Mac and save them to the Desktop. You can even print them and take them with you, if necessary.

1 From the Finder's Application window, open Stickies. Read what's offered.

2 Verify Stickies is showing on the Menu bar and click File>New Note.

3 Type your note.

4 Click Font>Show Fonts. If desired, choose a new Font Size.

5 To quit Stickies, click Stickies>Quit Stickies.

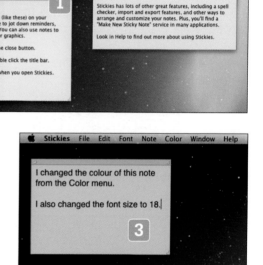

 HOT TIP: When Stickies is active, use the keyboard shortcut Command + N to create a note quickly.

 ALERT: If, in step 3, Stickies is not showing on the Menu bar, click any note to make the application active.

 HOT TIP: To close a note, click the Close button on it. That's a very small button you may not be able to see, but it's in the top left corner of each note. You'll be prompted to save or discard the note.

Play a game of chess

You don't need a partner to play a game of chess: you can play a game against your Mac. Be careful, though, that Mac guy is pretty good!

1 In the Finder, click Applications.

2 Open Chess.

3 Use your mouse to click and drag a chess piece to play it.

4 Wait while your Mac makes a move.

5 In between moves, take time to explore the Menu bar options.

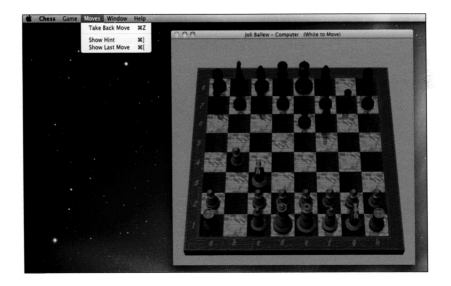

 DID YOU KNOW?
You can take back your last move from the Moves menu.

 HOT TIP: Click Game and Save As to save your game. Then you can quit Chess and return to the game when you have time.

 HOT TIP: Click Window and click Zoom to increase the size of the chess board for easier viewing.

Get a free game from the App Store

The App Store is a store where you can get apps (applications). To use the App Store you need to have set up an Apple ID, which you've probably done. If you haven't, don't worry, you'll be prompted if need be.

1 From the Finder's Application window, open the App Store.

2 At the top of the App Store window, click Categories.

3 Click Games.

4 Scroll down until you can see Top Free.

5 Locate a free game you'd like to play and click Free, then Install App.

6 Type your Apple ID and password and click Sign In.

7 Watch the app install on the Dock.

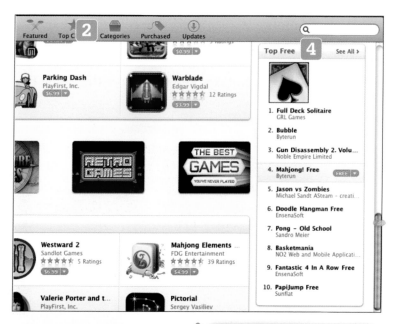

ALERT: The App Store, along with a few other applications, requires you to be online to use it.

HOT TIP: While in the App Store, explore Featured, Top Charts, Additional Categories, and more.

ALERT: If you purchase an app, the price of the app will be charged to the credit card you used to set up your App Store account, or it will be deducted from any gift card you've input.

? DID YOU KNOW?
An icon for the App Store is on the Dock by default, so if you haven't moved it, you can open the App Store there.

Play a game from the App Store

Once you've downloaded and installed a game from the App Store, you can play it. By default, the new game is on the Dock, but you can also access from the Applications window.

1 Locate the game you downloaded in the previous section and open it.

2 Read any introductory materials and any instructions offered from the Menu bar.

3 Click Play Game, New Game, or something similar.

4 While in a game and while learning to play, look for Hint buttons or instructions.

HOT TIP: Most games offer the chance to save the game, quit the app and return to the game when time allows. Check the File menu and others for this option.

? DID YOU KNOW?
If you have an iPhone, iPad or other compatible i-device, you can sync the app to it and play it there.

Explore the iTunes Store

The App Store offers apps and the iTunes Store offers 'tunes' (and movies, TV shows, podcasts and more). The iTunes application also lets you manage your media library, create playlists and view media you've obtained from the iTunes Store. You'll need to be connected to the Internet to shop at the iTunes Store.

1 Open iTunes from the Dock or the Finder's Application window.

2 In the left pane, click iTunes Store.

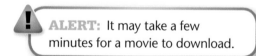

3 At the top of the iTunes window, click Music, then Movies. Explore the titles.

4 To make a purchase:

   a. Click the item.

   b. Click the Buy (or Rent) button, as applicable.

   c. Type your password.

   d. Click Buy.

5 In the left pane, click Music or Movies to access your purchases.

! ALERT: It may take a few minutes for a movie to download.

? DID YOU KNOW?
iTunes on an iPad or iPhone (or other compatible i-device) doesn't offer all of the features found on iTunes on your Mac. On these devices, it's just a link to the iTunes Store and nothing else.

🔥 HOT TIP: Explore Books and iTunes U to feed your intellectual side!

Play a song in iTunes

If you have purchased music from the iTunes Store, ripped CDs you own or otherwise made music available on your Mac, you'll find that music in iTunes. iTunes lets you play your music and create playlists, among other things.

1 Open iTunes.

2 In the left pane, click Music. (Change the view if desired.)

3 Locate the song to play. What you see may differ from what's shown here.

4 Click or double-click the song to play it.

5 Explore the controls available to rewind, pause/play and fast-forward.

6 Click All Albums to return to the current view.

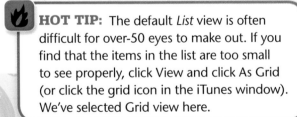

🔥 **HOT TIP:** The default *List* view is often difficult for over-50 eyes to make out. If you find that the items in the list are too small to see properly, click View and click As Grid (or click the grid icon in the iTunes window). We've selected Grid view here.

? **DID YOU KNOW?**
You can view and access any media you've purchased from the iTunes Store from the iTunes Purchased option in the left pane.

WHAT DOES THIS MEAN?

Rip a CD: Copy the CD – you copy the music files to your Mac.

Take a screenshot with the Grab utility

There's a folder in the Applications window called Utilities. Utilities offers all kinds of things you'll probably never (or rarely) use, but there is one that can be quite useful on a regular basis. That's the Grab utility. You can use Grab to take a picture of anything on your screen.

1 Open Applications and open Utilities.

2 Open Grab.

3 Notice the Menu bar now offers Grab options.

4 Click Capture and click Selection. (Note the other options.)

5 Use your mouse to drag to select a particular part of the screen, perhaps part of the Utilities window.

6 To save the screen capture that appears, from the Menu bar click File>Save As and complete the saving process.

Utilities **1**

Grab **2**

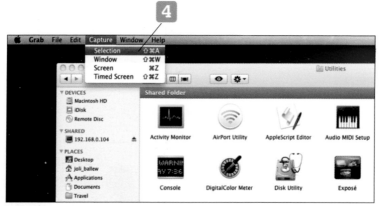

Set up FaceTime

FaceTime lets you hold video chats with others. The people you want to video chat with must have an iPad 2, iPhone 4, iPod Touch or a Mac with a video camera and FaceTime. You must have a webcam installed and be connected to the Internet.

1 From the Applications window, open FaceTime.

2 Sign in with your Apple ID or opt to create an account.

3 Type or select the email account to use to be notified of FaceTime calls and click Next.

4 You must now locate a contact from your contact list to communicate with or add a new contact. One way is to:

   a. Click Contacts in the FaceTime window.

   b. Click the + sign in the All Contacts list.

   c. Type the desired information.

   d. Click Done.

? DID YOU KNOW?
iPad 2, iPhone 4 and iPod Touch users must be connected to a Wi-Fi network to use FaceTime.

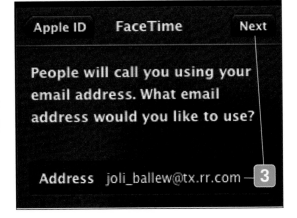

! ALERT: You can't hold a FaceTime conversation with a contact unless you can see a video camera by their name. This means they have FaceTime and a camera and are available.

Make a video call with FaceTime

Once you've set up FaceTime with your Apple ID and password, and configured an email address to use for invitations, all you need to do now is to locate the contact in your contact list and initiate the call. Of course, the person you want to call has to be online and available, so you may want to contact them ahead of time and let them know when you'll be calling, but other than that it's pretty easy.

1 Open FaceTime.

2 If necessary, log in.

3 Click Favorites, Recents or Contacts to locate the person to video chat with.

4 If the user has a video camera by their name, click it to start the video call.

5 To end the call, click End.

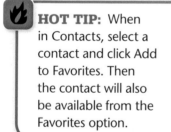

HOT TIP: When in Contacts, select a contact and click Add to Favorites. Then the contact will also be available from the Favorites option.

ALERT: You can't send someone a video of yourself without their permission. If you are having trouble making a call to a person, make sure they know you're trying to call them via FaceTime and let them know when you'll be calling.

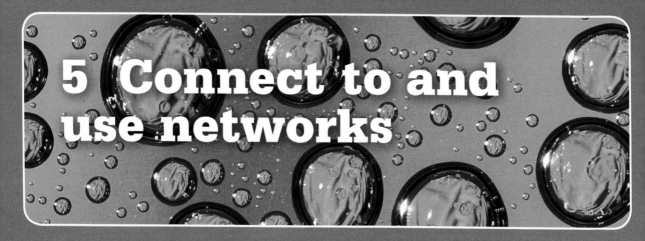

5 Connect to and use networks

Introduction

All Macs can connect to networks. If you have a Desktop computer, you'll probably connect to your own home network or one where you work. If you have a laptop, the networks you connect to may include those at home or work, as well as free, open networks at coffee shops and libraries. Once you're connected to a network, if there are shared files and folders, or printers or other hardware available, you may have permission to access and use them.

You can also share the data you've saved to your Mac with others. You can do this in two ways: you can create a user account for another user and let that user log on to your Mac directly, or you can let a user access the folders you've shared over the network. Whatever you decide, you get to set who can access what by configuring the user accounts and shared folders you've created.

It's important to note that in this book, we're using a Mac OS X 10.6 version. Therefore, what's detailed here may not work exactly as described if you're using an earlier version. It should be close, though.

Connect to a private network wirelessly

One of the most common networking scenarios is a personal network that incorporates a networking device that allows wireless connections. Often, this is a router. Users connect to each other and to the internet through this hardware, and using the network can share printers, data, and scanners, among other things.

1 Turn on your Mac within range of a wireless network.

2 If you are prompted to join the network, click the prompt and type the required credentials.

3 If you are not prompted to join the network:

   a. Open System Preferences from the Dock or the Applications window.
   b. Open Network.

   c. Click the lock and enter the proper credentials, if necessary, to unlock the settings options.

   d. Click AirPort (Off) and then click Turn AirPort On, if necessary.

? DID YOU KNOW?
You can search for anything from the Menu bar, even System Preferences.

🔥 HOT TIP: Your Mac should be less than 50m from the wireless router if you're indoors and less than 100m if outdoors.

e. Under Network Name, select the network to join.

f. Type in any required information, such as the password used to secure the wireless network.

4 Verify you're connected to the network in the left pane of the Network window.

WHAT DOES THIS MEAN?

Router: A piece of hardware that is used to connect computers to form a network, often for the purpose of sharing a single internet connection, printers and data.

Connect to a private network with Ethernet

Ethernet is a common way to connect a computer to an existing network. You'll need an Ethernet cable and will use it to physically connect your Mac to the Ethernet-enabled hardware. This is called a 'wired' connection.

1 Open System Preferences, open Network and click Ethernet.

2 If you see Cable Unplugged (as shown here):

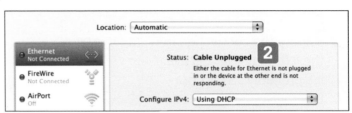

   a. Connect one end of an Ethernet cable to your Mac.

   b. Connect the other end of the cable to your router or other network hardware.

3 Wait while the network is automatically configured.

 ALERT: Do not connect your Mac directly to another computer; connect only to a router or other networking hardware.

WHAT DOES THIS MEAN?

DHCP: A technology that automatically assigns the proper network address to your computer so it can join the network. Without this technology, you'd have to input the various entries manually.

Join a Windows workgroup

You can join a network and gain access to the Internet, but if you want to join an existing Windows workgroup, you'll have to perform a few more steps. You won't be able to share data with the workgroup computers (or certainly not easily) until you join.

1 Open System Preferences and then Network. If applicable, click the lock to enable changes.

2 Choose the connection in the left pane that's active. It's probably AirPort or Ethernet.

3 Click Advanced.

4 From the WINS tab, type a name for your Mac or keep the one that's assigned already.

5 Type the name of the Windows workgroup to join.

6 Click OK and click Apply.

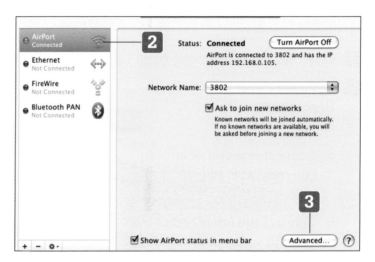

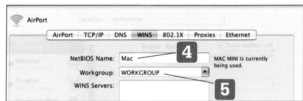

 ALERT: It may take a few minutes for you to see other compatible computers in the Finder. You won't see the Windows computers until you've 'mounted' them, as detailed next.

WHAT DOES THIS MEAN?

Workgroup: A Windows term for a group of computers all belonging to the same network. Common workgroup names are MSHOME and WORKGROUP.

Connect to a computer on the network

If, after 5 minutes or so, you don't see the computers on your network in the Finder, you'll need to 'mount' them. In this example we'll show how to mount a Windows computer so that you have access to it from your Mac.

1 Open the Finder.

2 From the Menu bar, click Go.

3 Click Connect to Server.

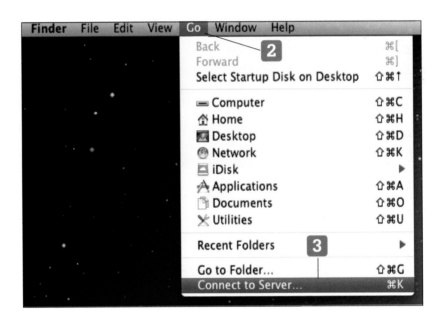

ALERT: You may have to manually connect (mount) a networked computer each time you boot your Mac, depending on other settings and the circumstances.

 HOT TIP: You can create an alias for a networked folder by right-clicking the folder and selecting Make Alias or by choosing Make Alias from the File menu on the Menu bar.

4 Keep **smb://** and replace the rest with the name of the Windows computer you want to connect to.

5 Click the + sign to add the server to your list of Favorite Servers.

6 Select the server in the list and click Connect.

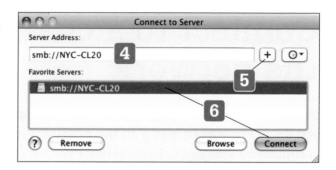

7 Input the administrator name and password used on the Windows computer.

8 Select the folder to connect to and click OK.

9 An icon for the Windows computer will appear in the Finder. Click it to see the shared folders.

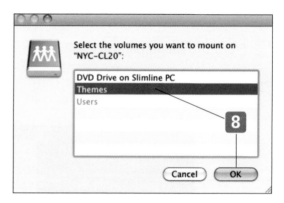

ALERT: When you type a user name and password in step 6, do not use your Mac user account and password. Instead, use an administrator account name and password on the Windows computer.

ALERT: Unless you specify otherwise in Accounts, under the tab Login Items, you'll have to mount the server after every reboot of your Mac.

? DID YOU KNOW?
You can delete a server from the Favorite Servers list by clicking the server and clicking Remove.

Connect to a public network wirelessly

When you take your laptop to a public place such as a coffee shop, pub, hotel, or the like, you may find that the establishment offers free Wi-Fi that enables you to connect to the Internet. These types of networks are called 'hotspots' and are generally unsecured, meaning they do not require you to input a password.

1 Get within range of a free, unsecured Wi-Fi network.

2 When you see a prompt about joining that network, click it to join.

3 If you do not see a prompt:

    a. Open System Preferences and click Network.

    b. Click AirPort.

    c. If Airport is turned off, turn it on.

    d. If Ask to join new networks is not enabled, enable it.

    e. If prompted to apply the changes, click Apply.

    f. When you see the prompt to join the network, select it.

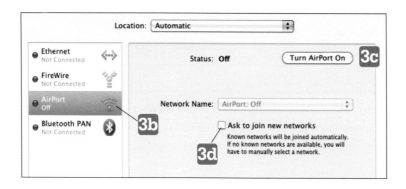

ALERT: Some establishments *will* require you to buy a beer, get a library card or rent a room to gain access to the network, and in some places will even require a password to make sure you do. Most don't, though.

ALERT: If you can't make changes to the existing settings, click the lock in the bottom left corner of the Network window. Input your administrator name and password as required.

Allow another user to log on to your Mac

An easy way to share data with others is to create a user account for them. Then they can log on to your computer using that account and access what you've shared. (You'll learn how to share specific folders later in this chapter.)

1 Open System Preferences.

2 Click Accounts.

3 If necessary, click the lock so that you can make changes.

4 Click the + sign just above the lock icon.

5 Fill in the required information for the new user and click Create Account.

6 Answer any additional prompts as required.

ALERT: If you create a user account for the person (or people) you want to share with before you actually share anything, you will avoid potential sharing problems later.

 DID YOU KNOW?

You can create a user account for a Windows user on your network and later share files with them over the network through System Preferences>Sharing>File Sharing>Options.

DID YOU KNOW?

In Accounts, you can click your user name to change your password or enable login items. You can select other accounts, too, provided you're an administrator, and assign parental controls, among other things.

Enable File Sharing

Once you're connected to your home network you can share data with others who are also part of that network. For instance, you may have a folder on your Mac containing pictures from a recent holiday and you want your spouse to be able to view those pictures from his own computer, through the network. There are two steps to achieving this. The first is to enable File Sharing; the second is to choose which folder to share and configure sharing preferences.

1 Open System Preferences.

2 Open Sharing.

3 Place a tick by File Sharing and click Options.

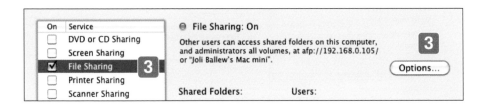

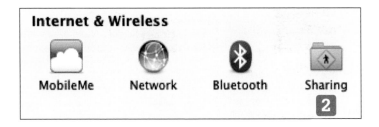

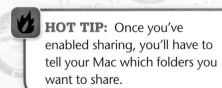

ALERT: Remember, if you can't make changes to the existing settings, click the lock in the bottom left corner and enter an administrator's name and password.

HOT TIP: Once you've enabled sharing, you'll have to tell your Mac which folders you want to share.

4 To share files with other Apple computers, tick Share files and folders using AFP.

5 To share files and folders with Linux and Unix-based computers, tick Share files and folders using FTP.

6 To share files and folders with Windows computers, tick Share files and folders using SMB (Windows). Then:

a. Place a tick by each user you want to allow access.

b. Input the password for the user account.

7 Click Done.

ALERT: When allowing Windows users to access your Mac via a network, you must enter the password they use on their Windows computer in step 6b.

ALERT: Sharing with Lion is different from this, but the concept is the same. Choose what kinds of computers you'll share with and which users have access.

Access a Mac's shared folders from a Windows computer

If you've shared a folder with a Windows computer on your network, you may need to show the Windows user how to access those files. On a windows computer:

1 Open Windows Explorer.

2 Expand Network.

3 Expand the Mac computer.

4 Browse the shared folders.

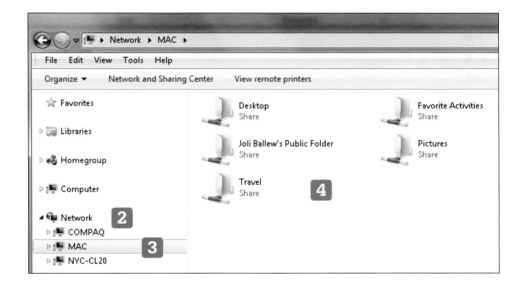

HOT TIP: Windows users can right-click and drag any shared folder from this window to the Desktop to create a shortcut for easier access.

ALERT: If you've given the Windows (or any other) user Read & Write access to a folder, that user can edit, delete and otherwise manipulate the data inside the shared folders.

Enable DVD or CD sharing

You may have noticed in the Sharing window that you can share more than files – you can share your Mac's DVD or CD drive, a connected printer and more. By default, you'll have to approve requests by users to access the drive, but you can disable that.

1 Open System Preferences.

2 Open Sharing.

3 Select DVD or CD Sharing.

4 If desired, deselect Ask me before allowing others to use my DVD drive.

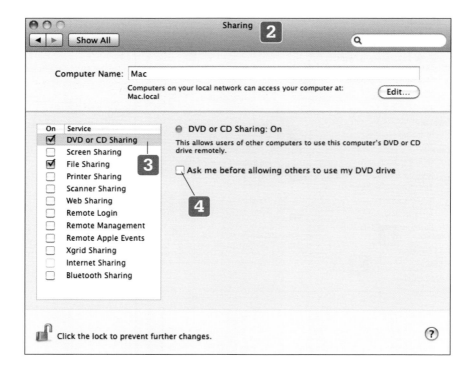

HOT TIP: Remember, if you can't make changes you'll have to click the lock icon in the bottom left corner and type in your administrator password.

ALERT: As with other sharing tasks, it may take a few minutes for the shared drive to appear on other computers on the network.

Share a printer

You enable printer sharing in the same way as you enable DVD or CD sharing. However, with printer sharing you can add users and configure printer preferences, too.

1 Open System Preferences and open Sharing.

2 Place a tick by Printer Sharing.

3 Select the printer to configure under Printers.

4 To limit who can print, click the + sign under Users, then:

    a. Add a user from the list.

    b. Click Select.

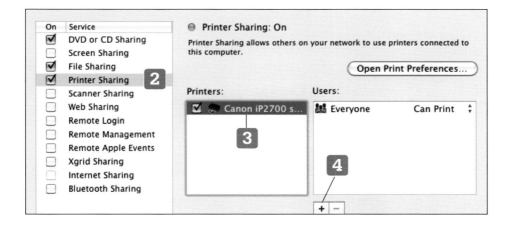

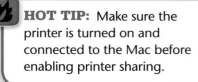**HOT TIP:** Make sure the printer is turned on and connected to the Mac before enabling printer sharing.

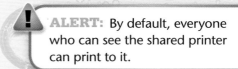**ALERT:** By default, everyone who can see the shared printer can print to it.

Access a shared printer

You'll access the shared printer when you're ready to print to it. You can locate the printer from any application's Print dialogue box, even on a Windows computer as shown here. Accessing the shared printer is detailed here using Microsoft Word, but the same process will usually work for other programs.

1 Click the File button and click Print.

2 Choose the shared printer.

3 Configure settings as desired, then click OK.

4 Click Print.

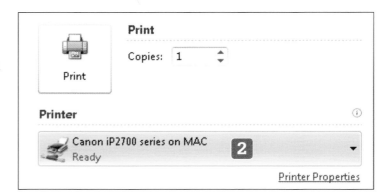

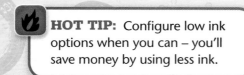 **HOT TIP:** Configure low ink options when you can – you'll save money by using less ink.

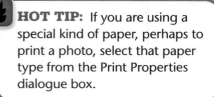 **HOT TIP:** If you are using a special kind of paper, perhaps to print a photo, select that paper type from the Print Properties dialogue box.

6 Surf the Web with Safari

Introduction

Safari is an application that comes with all Macs that lets you browse the Internet. That's why it's called a *web browser*; you use it to browse the Web! You can do more than browse, though. You can access tools such as Zoom and Speech to make the web easier to use, and create bookmarks for pages you'd like to open again. There are built-in tools to help keep you safe while you surf the web too, although you still have to use a little common sense to stay out of trouble. We'll start off by exploring Safari's interface.

Explore the Safari interface

When you open Safari the first time, you'll probably be taken to Apple's home page. You can quickly jump to other webpages though, and you can easily search for information on any topic from the search window. Open Safari and note these features and others.

1 From the Dock, open Safari.

2 Locate the following items:

   a. Minimise Safari.

   b. Back and Forward buttons.

   c. Bookmarks bar and Bookmarks list.

🔥 **HOT TIP:** If you don't see the Safari icon on the Dock, search for it from the Menu bar (click the magnifying glass and type Safari).

❓ **DID YOU KNOW?**

If Safari is not on the Dock and you want it there, open the Finder, click Applications and drag Safari from the Applications window to the Dock. (Safari will still be available from the Applications window.)

d. Thumbnail view.

e. Address bar.

f. Search window.

g. Add Bookmark icon.

h. Refresh.

i. Scroll bars.

j. Drop-down lists.

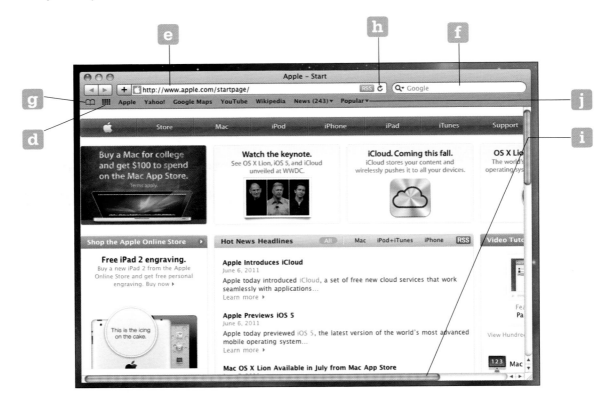

Surf the Internet

The term 'surf the internet' means to explore webpages, moving from one to another using web links or search results. You can also type in the address of a webpage in the Address bar, or access pages from any bookmark lists you have available to surf from page to page. Surfing is also referred to as browsing or navigating the web.

1 Open Safari. If you don't see a webpage, from the Bookmark bar click Apple.

2 Move the mouse over the page and when the cursor becomes a hand, click with the mouse.

3 If you click a link to a video, click the Play button to play the video.

4 Click the Back button or click another link in the Bookmark bar.

5 In the Address bar, type www.weather.com. Press Enter on the keyboard.

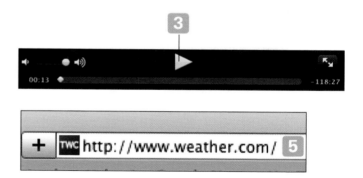

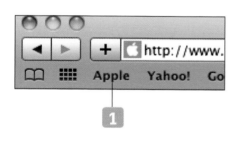

? DID YOU KNOW?
You don't always have to type the http:// part of a web address – Safari knows where you're going!

! ALERT: If you are prompted to download something, don't. You'll learn how to stay safe on the Web and download items later in this chapter.

? DID YOU KNOW?
Practically every webpage offers at least one link to another page, but if you don't see one, you can always click the Back button to return to the page you were on previously.

HOT TIP: You can continue exploring as you wish, but for now visit only reputable and known websites (such as www. bbc.co.uk and www.weather. com) and avoid clicking any ads.

Search for something specific

Sometimes you'll want to search for information on a particular topic, perhaps the latest score in a football match or potential side effects of a drug you've been prescribed. You may want directions for doing something, such as installing a new dishwasher or catching a raccoon. Whatever you want to find, you can find it on the Web.

1 Open Safari and click inside the Spotlight Search window.

2 Type the keywords you'll use to locate the information you want (*how to catch a raccoon* or *what are the side effects of Niaspan*).

3 If you see a result you like in the drop-down list, click it.

4 If you don't see what you want in the results, click Enter on the keyboard.

5 Click any result, noting the web link you'll navigate to.

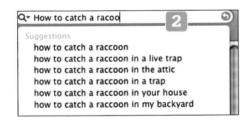

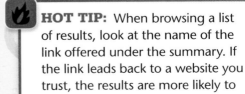

ALERT: Be careful not to believe everything you read. Just because it's on the Web doesn't make it true.

? DID YOU KNOW?

Often you'll see the results you want even if you misspell a word in the Search box, don't complete your query or search for something obscure.

HOT TIP: When browsing a list of results, look at the name of the link offered under the summary. If the link leads back to a website you trust, the results are more likely to be reliable.

Zoom in on a webpage

If you have trouble viewing search results or what's on a webpage, you can zoom in on it. This will make everything on the page larger. It may be just what your aching over-50 eyes have been searching for! There are two ways to zoom in on a page:

- Hold down the Command key (or the Windows key if applicable) and press the + sign. Repeat as often as you need to. (Press Command and – to zoom back out.)

- Click View, then click Zoom In. This will zoom in on everything, including images.

ALERT: By default, when you zoom in on a page, you'll zoom in on the images, too. Sometimes they'll distort, but often you don't need to zoom in on the images anyway, only the text. If you want to change the default so that the Zoom command increases the text size only, click View and click Zoom Text Only.

 HOT TIP: If you're still having trouble viewing what Safari has to offer, try Window>Zoom from the Menu bar.

 HOT TIP: Make sure the Safari window is maximised and drag to enlarge the window even more from the bottom right corner of Safari to make the window as large as possible.

 DID YOU KNOW?

We like the Bookmark bar, but you can hide it if you wish. This will increase Safari's screen size a little. Choose Hide Bookmarks Bar from the View menu to do this.

View thumbnails of websites

Thumbnail view, if you can see it clearly, is a brilliant method for accessing websites you access often. What you see in thumbnail view changes to reflect your surfing habits and makes accessing those sites simple.

1 Click the thumbnails icon in Safari.

2 Verify that Top Sites is selected.

3 Click any site to go there.

4 Click the thumbnails icon again.

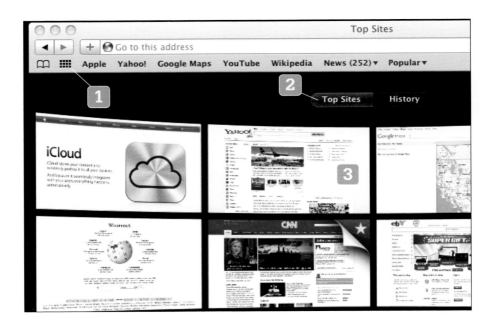

HOT TIP: In thumbnail view, note the Spotlight Search window at the bottom of the page. Type a word here to search the pages in your History list.

DID YOU KNOW?
Zooming is disabled when in thumbnail view. What you see is what you get.

5 Click History.

6 Click any webpage and click it again to go there.

5

CNN.com – Breaking News, U.S., World, Weather, Entertainment & Video News
http://www.cnn.com/
Today

HOT TIP: While in thumbnail view, under Top Sites click Edit to delete unwanted thumbnails. (Click Done when you've finished.)

Enable tab browsing

You can have more than one webpage open at a time by enabling tab browsing. Once multiple tabs are open you can click the tab to go to the page while leaving the other pages open and available. Here, we've opened three tabs: the Apple home page, Facebook and the BBC home page.

1 From the Menu bar, click Safari and then click Preferences. (Safari must be active.)

2 Click Tabs.

3 Choose Open pages in tabs instead of windows: Automatically.

4 Tick When a new tab or window opens, make it active.

5 While on any webpage, hold down the Command key and then click a link on the page. Note the new tab.

6 To close a tab, position your mouse over it and click the X that appears.

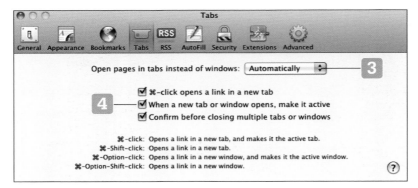

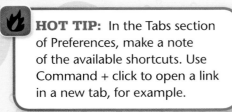
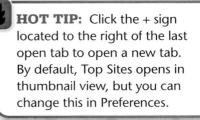

Let Safari read to you

You can get Safari to read to you if you have trouble reading what's on a webpage. Unfortunately, there's no keyboard shortcut for starting the speech feature, so you'll have to access it from Safari's Edit menu.

1 With Safari active and a webpage available, click the Edit menu.

2 Click Speech>Start Speaking.

3 To stop narration, click Speech> Stop Speaking.

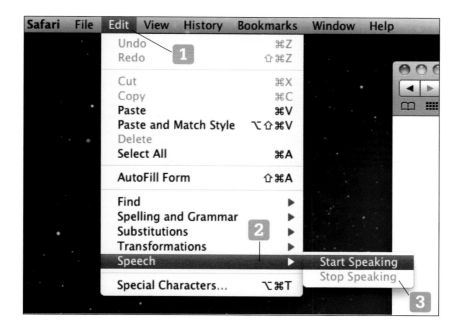

? DID YOU KNOW?

There are other features available if you're visually impaired. Try VoiceOver, Screen Magnification, Cursor Magnification and High Contrast, among others. Search for these features from the Spotlight Search window on the Menu bar.

🔥 HOT TIP: If you don't see the Edit menu shown here, click Safari's title bar. Remember, an application has to be active for its options to appear in the Menu bar.

Use Safari Reader

Sometimes, when you come across an article you want to read on the Internet, the elements included with the article are distracting. If you have a visual impairment or if you use VoiceOver when surfing the Web (and it tries to read these elements), keep an eye out for the Reader icon in Safari's Address bar. If you see it, you can click it to view the article with fewer distractions.

1 Visit www.wikipedia.com.

2 Browse the articles by clicking links on any page.

3 When you see Reader in the Address bar, click it.

4 Use the controls to zoom in or out as desired, to email the page or to print it, or to close the Reader window.

Big Bend area of Florida on June 13. Alberto then moved through eastern Georgia, North Carolina, and Virginia as a tropical depression before becoming extratropical on June 14.

Across the Western Caribbean, the storm produced heavy rainfall, causing some minor damage. In Florida, a moderate storm tide caused coastal damage and flooding, whi... ...nds produced several tornadoes. ...ctly responsible

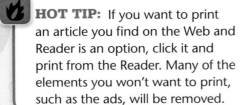

HOT TIP: If the controls disappear, position your mouse at the bottom of the Reader page. They'll reappear.

HOT TIP: If you want to print an article you find on the Web and Reader is an option, click it and print from the Reader. Many of the elements you won't want to print, such as the ads, will be removed.

DID YOU KNOW?
You can click the X in the controls to close the Reader or simply click Reader again in the Address bar.

Create a bookmark

There are some webpages you'll visit often, perhaps Facebook, a local news website, or a fan page for your favourite football team. You can use thumbnail view to access them, or you can bookmark those pages. When you bookmark a page, it will be available in the Bookmarks list, on the Bookmarks bar or in a folder you select or create.

1 Navigate to a webpage you'd like to bookmark.

2 Click the + sign to the left of the Address bar.

3 Type a name for the bookmark or keep the one provided.

4 Use the drop-down list to decide where to save the bookmark.

5 Click Add.

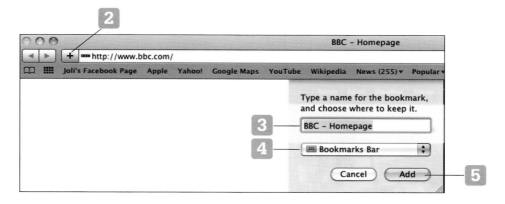

ALERT: You can choose Bookmark menu from the drop-down list in step 4, but if you make that a habit your bookmarks list will eventually become cluttered. It's best to create your own bookmark folders (detailed next) and save your bookmarks in them.

HOT TIP: Don't save too many bookmarks to the Bookmarks bar; save only those you access on a daily basis.

DID YOU KNOW?
If you save a bookmark to the Bookmark menu, you can click the Bookmarks option on the Menu bar or the Bookmarks icon in the Safari window to access it.

Create your own bookmark folder

You'll collect bookmarks, so it's best to get organised now in preparation for what you'll amass over the lifetime of your Mac. You can start by thinking about the kinds of bookmarks you'll keep and then create folders to represent them. You might create folders named Travel, Health, Reference and Retirement, among others.

1 With Safari open and active, from the Menu bar, click Bookmarks and Add Bookmark Folder. Type a name for the folder and hit the Return or Enter key on the keyboard.

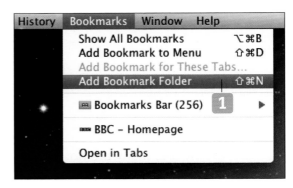

2 Repeat to add all of the desired folders.

3 Browse to any webpage to bookmark.

4 Click the + sign to add a bookmark.

5 Choose the appropriate folder to hold the bookmark.

6 Click add.

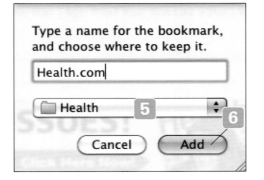

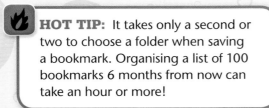

Stay safe on the Web

Although Safari will warn you when you try to access a fraudulent website (one that's been reported, anyway), prompt you to verify you want to send secured information away from a secure website when applicable, and block pop-up ads, among other things, you still have to be very careful when surfing the Web. Here are a few things to remember:

- If you are prompted by your Mac to input a password while surfing the Web, think twice. This means you're about to download something and downloads can contain viruses and other harmful code.

- When inputting credit card information, make sure the address in the Address bar starts with https://. That means it's secure.

- Don't give your login name and password to an application (such as one you might find on Facebook) unless you've researched it and determined the application is safe. (Many are; many are not.)

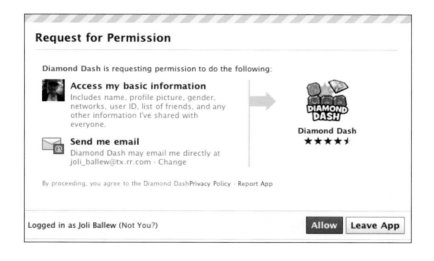

 HOT TIP: When you've finished using Safari, for good measure click Safari and click Quit Safari.

 ALERT: If you let others use your computer with your login name, they can easily send email as you, update your social status, download harmful content, and more. It's best to create user accounts for others who can use your computer and log out when you aren't using it yourself.

Download Flash Player

Although we suggest you stay away from most downloads, there are programs you'll need. For instance, you'll need to download Flash Player to watch certain web videos. Or you may want to purchase something from Apple such as an OS update, QuickTime Pro, or iWork. The download process is the same for all of them.

1 Locate something you want to download and click the Download link.

2 Click the Install option. You may see this option in more than one place.

3 When presented with the warning box, click Open to continue.

4 If applicable, perform any preinstallation tasks, such as agreeing to Terms of Service.

5 Click Install.

6 Type your password and click OK.

7 Wait while the program installs.

Download Adobe Flash Player

Adobe Flash Player
Macintosh OS X
Different operating system or browser?

Learn more | System requirements | Distribute Flash Player

Adobe Flash Player version 10.3.181.26
Universal Binary for Macs | 6.08 MB

Browser: Safari, Firefox, Opera
Download time estimate: 7 minutes @ 56K modem

⬇ Download now — 1

ALERT: It's often difficult to know whether a download is safe or not. The best way to find out is to read reviews and search the internet for user comments and complaints.

ALERT: You may be prompted to close related programs before installing a program. If so, click the title bar of the application to make it active, then from the Menu bar quit the application.

? DID YOU KNOW?
Downloading and installing an application are two separate things. Once a download is complete you must still perform the installation.

Explore Safari's Preferences options

When Safari is active, click Safari>Preferences to make changes to the program. You can change the search engine from Google to something else, change the start page from Apple to something you like better, set a minimum font size, and more. Here are our top Preferences changes; you can decide whether they are yours, too.

- Click the General tab to change the home page.

- Click the Appearance tab to increase the standard font size.

- Click the Advanced tab to choose a minimum font size for all webpages.

- Click the Advanced tab to enable *Press Tab to highlight each item on a webpage.*

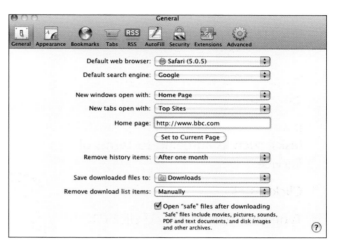

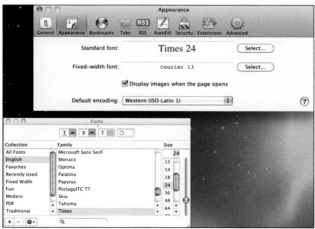

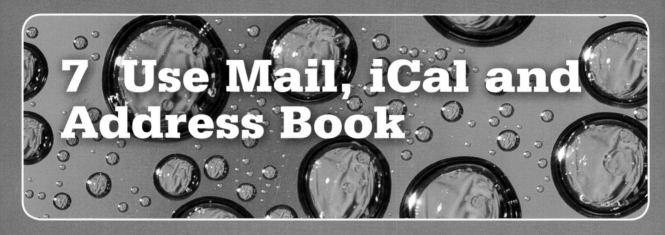

7 Use Mail, iCal and Address Book

Introduction

You have two main options for accessing your email from your Mac. You can log on to your email provider's website using Safari, or you can set up and use Mail. We prefer Mail over Safari because it's easy to save and organise email, attach pictures and other data to outgoing mail, and review what you've sent and saved. You can also manage several email accounts from a single interface, so there's no back and forth when you need to check multiple mail accounts. Mail also integrates nicely with iCal (a calendar application) and Address Book (a contact management application), both included with your Mac along with Mail.

Set up an email account in Mail

You have to configure Mail with your email account and password before you can use it to retrieve your email. Sometimes this is easy; other times, you'll have to call your Internet service provider (ISP) or research the settings on the Web. The very first time you open Mail you'll be prompted to input the required information.

1 Open Mail. If prompted to set up an account skip to step 3.

2 If you aren't prompted to set up an account or want to set up a second account, click File>Add Account.

3 Type or accept your name and type your email address and password.

4 Click Continue.

5 If Mail can configure the account automatically, you'll be prompted to click Create; do so. Otherwise, skip to the next section.

6 You'll be able to see easily when you have new email from the Dock.

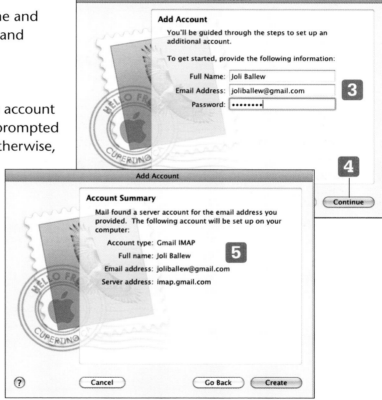

Input advanced account information

Sometimes when you add an account, Mail can't configure it automatically and asks you to input additional information. If you see the prompt here, choose to set up your email account manually.

1 If prompted during account set-up, click Setup Manually.

2 Leave POP selected unless you're positive you need to select something else.

Mail cannot send your password securely to the server.

You can continue without a secured password, which could put your password at risk. Alternatively, you can manually set up your account.

Do you want to continue without a secured password?

1 (Setup Manually)   (Cancel)   (Continue)

3 Fill in the required information. You will probably have to contact your ISP.

4 Click Continue.

5 Continue working through the screens offered. What you see and input will differ depending on your email provider's requirements.

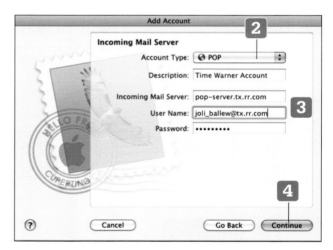

Add Account

Incoming Mail Server

Account Type: POP

Description: Time Warner Account

Incoming Mail Server: pop-server.tx.rr.com

User Name: joli_ballew@tx.rr.com

Password: ••••••••

 (Cancel)   (Go Back)   (Continue)

⚠ **ALERT:** You must input the information exactly as it is provided to you by your ISP. If you get errors after you create the account, call your ISP and get them to talk you through it.

🔥 **HOT TIP:** Some email providers require you to enable various security features during account creation. If you encounter any problems, call your ISP for help or search for the proper settings on the Web.

Reply to and forward email

Once your account is set up correctly, email will arrive automatically. If you've configured more than one email account, you'll see more than one listing under Mailboxes. To reply to or forward an email, you must select it first.

1 Click the desired inbox.

2 Click any email to respond to or forward.

3 Click Reply, Reply All or Forward.

4 If you clicked Forward in step 3, type the address of the person you'd like to forward the email to.

5 Type your response and click Send.

<hr>

DID YOU KNOW?
You can click Get Mail any time to see whether new mail has arrived at your ISP. Otherwise, Mail will automatically check for mail every 5 minutes on its own.

HOT TIP: Click Fonts when replying to an email to change the font size, colour and more.

HOT TIP: You can click Address in the New Message window to choose recipients from the Address Book. You'll learn how to add contacts to the Address Book at the end of this chapter.

DID YOU KNOW?
If an email in your Inbox appears in gold type instead of black, Mail thinks it is junk email. You can tell Mail it is not junk by clicking Not Junk at the top of the Mail window.

Open and view attachments

Some email comes with an item (or items) attached to it. It might be a word document, a photo, travel or show tickets, or a receipt, for instance. You may be able to take a 'quick look' at the attachment in Mail if it's a compatible file type, or you may want or need to open the attachment to view it, print it, share it or save it.

1 Open an email that contains an attachment.

2 If Quick Look is an option, click it. (Click X to close the Quick Look window.)

3 To open and view the attachment, click the attachment icon in the body of the email.

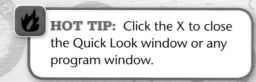

DID YOU KNOW?
You can click and hold the Save button to save a single attachment or multiple ones.

HOT TIP: Click the X to close the Quick Look window or any program window.

HOT TIP: While in Quick Look view, use the arrows to move among multiple attachments (useful when viewing photos, for instance).

Compose an email and attach a file

When you compose an email, you may want to attach something to it. Often, this will be a picture or a document, but it could be a short video or music file, too. You don't have to attach anything, though; you can simply create an email composed of text.

1 Click New Message in Mail.

2 In the To window, type the email address of the intended recipient.

3 Type a subject in the Subject line and your message in the body of the email.

4 If you want to attach a file:

   a. Click Attach.

   b. Locate the file to attach and click Choose File.

5 Complete the email and click Send.

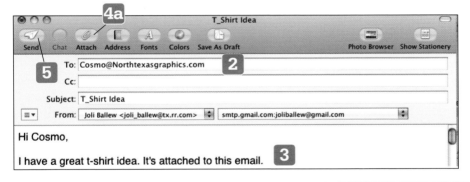

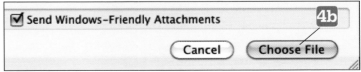

Insert a picture into an email

When you attach a picture as detailed in the previous section, it appears inside the body of the email. You can also drag a picture from the Finder to an email you're composing to attach (insert) it. Dragging can be very convenient and is detailed here.

1 Open the Finder and locate the photos to add to an email.

2 In Mail, click New Message.

3 Position the windows so you can drag from the Finder to the new email message.

4 Select the photos to add.

5 Drag the photos to the new email message and drop them there.

HOT TIP: If you want to save an email so you can complete it later (because you aren't ready to send it yet), click the red circle in the New Message window and when prompted, click Save. You can find the email later in Drafts, when you're ready to complete it.

DID YOU KNOW?
You can remove an attachment from an email by selecting it and pressing Delete on the keyboard.

DID YOU KNOW?
You hold down the Command key while selecting pictures to select more than one at a time. Here we've selected four.

HOT TIP: After you've dragged the photos to the new email, right-click or Command + click and choose View as Icon. This will make it easier to finish composing your email message by minimising the images you've added.

Manage junk email

Junk email is email you don't want from people you do not know. Email that Mail thinks is junk is shown in gold in your inbox. You'll want to train Mail so that it knows when an email is junk and when it isn't.

1. Click any email that Mail thinks is junk.

2. If it is not junk, click Not Junk. (You can also opt to load any images.)

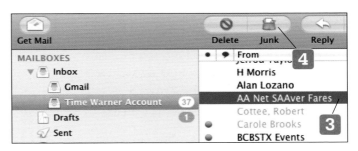

3. Click any email that Mail thinks is not junk.

4. If it is junk, click Junk.

5. To configure junk email preferences:

   a. Click Mail>Preferences from the Menu bar.

   b. Click Junk Mail.

   c. Configure junk mail options as desired.

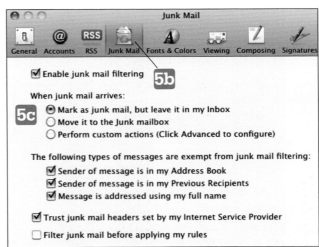

 HOT TIP: Need to write yourself a quick note? In Mail, click Note and start typing!

 HOT TIP: Once you've trained Mail about junk for a month or so, change the junk mail settings so that junk mail is moved to the Junk mailbox. (You can review what's there once a week or so.)

Make Mail easier to see

The fonts used throughout the Mail application are small. If it's hard to make out the names of the inboxes in the left pane or the information shown in the list of new messages, or it's hard to read incoming email because the font is just too small for your over-50 eyes to make out, you can enlarge the font. You can even change it!

1 Click Mail>Preferences from the Menu bar.

2 Click the Fonts & Colors tab.

3 Click Select to make a change to an item.

4 From the Fonts window, select a new font family, typeface and size.

5 Note the changes in the Mail window.

6 Repeat as desired.

HOT TIP: Command + click (or right-click) on the Subject or Date Received headings in Mail to add headings. Try Attachments and From, for starters.

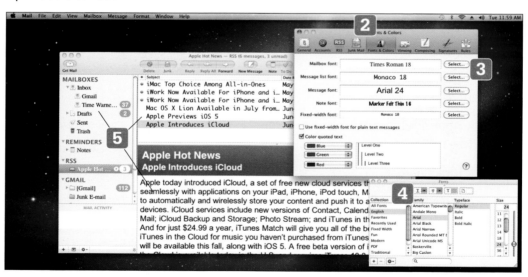

HOT TIP: It may be best to configure the same font attributes for the message list and the message body. It may be less distracting than if they were different, as shown here.

DID YOU KNOW?

After you've made changes, you simply click the red X in the top left corner of the Fonts and Preferences windows. Your changes will be applied automatically.

Create an event in iCal

iCal is a program included with your Mac that offers a place to manage a calendar and events. iCal is available from the Dock, but you can find it from the Applications window in Finder, too. Here, iCal is shown in Month view. You use iCal effectively by inputting information about upcoming events.

1 Click Month and browse to the date for your next event.

2 Click Command + N to create an event on that date.

3 Type a name for the event.

4 Click anywhere in the event window to edit the existing information or to set an alarm.

5 Click Done when you've finished.

WHAT DOES THIS MEAN?
Event: Can be an appointment, a date, a birthday or anniversary, among other things.

 ALERT: If you do not see the New Event window, double-click the new event.

 HOT TIP: You can press Command + click (right-click) and choose New Event to add an event to iCal, or you can choose New Event from the File menu on the Menu bar.

HOT TIP: Watch your calendar or set alarms to make sure you don't miss any events you've configured.

Share an event from iCal

To share an event you email it. You can email the event to yourself (for use on a smart phone, for instance) or to anyone else. Alternatively, you can 'invite' people to the event from inside the event window, shown in the previous section.

1 Locate an event in iCal.

2 Command + click or right-click and choose Mail Event.

3 Configure the email as desired and click Send.

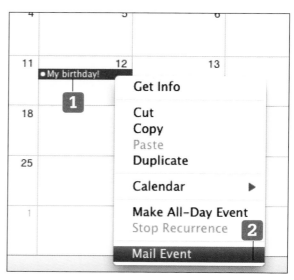

HOT TIP: If you work with iCal invitations a lot, change Mail preferences to add invitations to iCal 'Automatically'. By default, the setting is 'Never' (Mail>Preferences, General).

? DID YOU KNOW?
Many email programs can open iCal events, even on Windows computers, although not all can. If compatible, recipients can accept or decline your invitation from their email program and you'll receive a response.

? DID YOU KNOW?
In iCal, you can click the + sign at the bottom of the iCal window to add a calendar. By default, there is one configured named Work and one named Home, but you can create one named Travel, Gym, Golf, or some other activity.

Create a contact in Address Book

The Address Book, iCal and Mail (and iChat, too) all work together. As you may have guessed, the Address Book holds contact information for people you email or otherwise communicate with. The Address Book is located on the Dock by default, but if you've moved it you can find it in the Applications window from Finder.

1 Open Address Book.

2 In the middle pane, click the + sign to create a contact card.

3 Click and type the desired information. You can use the Tab key to move among entries.

4 When complete, click Edit.

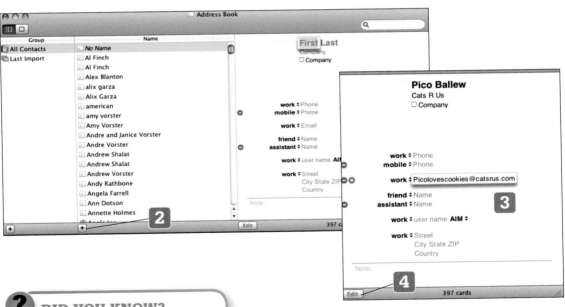

? DID YOU KNOW?

After you input your contacts' email addresses in the Address Book, you can click Address in any New Message window in Mail to access those addresses quickly and to use them in the To: line.

🔥 HOT TIP: To import existing addresses (that you've exported using another email program), open Address Book and click File>Import. Follow the prompts to locate and import those email addresses.

Edit a contact

Often contact information changes, or you decide to add an address or a picture for a contact (among other things). To edit a contact, simply select it and click Edit to enter the new information.

1 Locate the contact to edit in Address Book. (You can search for it, as shown here.)

2 Click Edit.

3 Click any entry in the card to edit it; consider double-clicking the empty picture placeholder.

4 Enter the desired information (or browse for a photo to set).

5 Click Edit when you've finished.

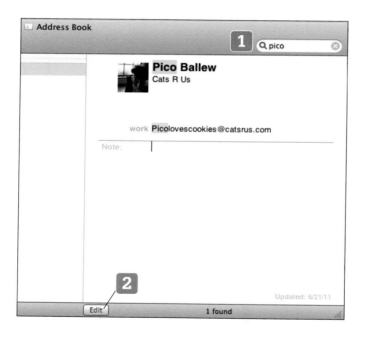

8 Upload, view and manage pictures

Introduction

You may already have some pictures on your Mac, and they are probably stored in the Pictures folder (with cryptic names such as DSCN0837.JPG). You may also have pictures on a camera, camera card, CD or DVD, or even a networked computer, that you'd like to put on your Mac. Beyond getting pictures on your Mac, though, you probably want to organise them, edit them and even share them. That's what you'll learn here.

Explore the Pictures folder

The Pictures folder is available in the Finder and is where you'll store your pictures. You may or may not have any pictures in there yet, but it's still good to explore the folder right at the start.

1 Open the Finder and click your user name in the left pane.

2 Open the Pictures folder.

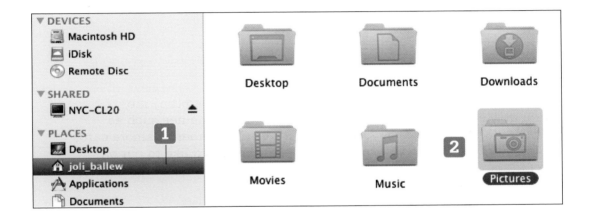

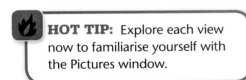

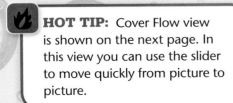

> 🔥 **HOT TIP:** Explore each view now to familiarise yourself with the Pictures window.

> 🔥 **HOT TIP:** Cover Flow view is shown on the next page. In this view you can use the slider to move quickly from picture to picture.

> ❓ **DID YOU KNOW?**
> When a picture is selected, you click the Preview icon to open it in a larger window (and click the X to close it).

3 Note the view options:

   a. View as icons.

   b. View as a list.

   c. View in columns.

   d. View as cover flow.

   e. Preview an image with Quick Look.

   f. Access contextual menu.

   g. Search.

Copy pictures from a camera or camera card

If you have a digital camera you can copy the pictures on it to your Mac. If you don't have many pictures on your Mac yet, this is a great way to add some.

1 Connect the camera using its USB cable or remove the camera card and insert it into your Mac's card reader.

2 Open Finder and select the device.

3 If applicable, open any folders and subfolders necessary to access the pictures.

4 To select all the pictures in a folder, click Edit>Select All.

5 To select some of the pictures in a folder hold down the Command key while selecting.

6 Click Edit>Copy Items.

7 Open the Pictures folder and click Edit>Paste Items.

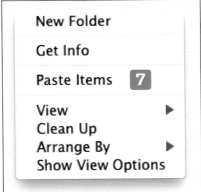

ALERT: If you've previously used iPhoto and told the program you wanted it to open when you inserted a camera card or digital camera, it will. However, you can still access the card from the Finder, as detailed here.

DID YOU KNOW?
There are lots of ways to import photos from a camera or camera card. You'll learn a few more options as you work through this chapter.

DID YOU KNOW?
The keyboard shortcut for Copy is Command + C; the keyboard shortcut for Paste is Command + V.

HOT TIP: If you like to drag and drop, open the Pictures window and the Device window. Then you can drag files from the device to the open folder instead of using Copy and Paste.

Copy pictures from a networked computer

If you set up a network as detailed in Chapter 5, you can copy pictures from shared folders on your networked computers and put them on your Mac. You have to be able to access the shared computer in the Finder before you start, a task also outlined in Chapter 5.

1 Open Finder.

2 Select the shared computer in the left pane.

3 Locate the folder that contains the pictures to copy by 'drilling into' the folders on the shared computer.

4 Select the pictures to copy.

5 Copy and paste the pictures using your preferred technique.

DID YOU KNOW?
After selecting pictures, you can drag them to your user name in the Finder, hold there, and then drag them over the Pictures folder and hold there, and finally drop them in the desired Pictures folder. This allows you to move pictures to subfolders without having to navigate to those subfolders beforehand.

HOT TIP: We've chosen Columns view here to show you how deep you may have to dig to locate pictures on a shared computer.

DID YOU KNOW?
Hold down the Shift key to select multiple, contiguous pictures. Just click the first in the list and then the last, and all of the pictures in between will also be selected.

Explore options for scanning pictures

If you have a scanner and pictures to scan, you have several options for doing so. It'll be up to you to decide which is best for you.

- Press the button on the scanner and use the scanner software.

- While in Preview (detailed later), choose File>Import from Scanner.

- Use a third-party program such as Photoshop Elements, which includes commands such as 'Import from Scanner'.

- Use the Mac's Image Capture program. It's in the Applications folder.

- Access and use a networked scanner.

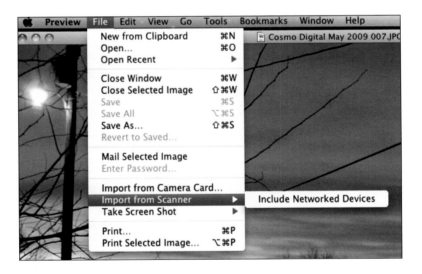

 HOT TIP: If you have old photos in a shoebox in the attic, get them down and start scanning! Future generations will thank you.

 ALERT: Your scanner has to be Mac-compatible, installed, connected and turned on in order to function. If you are having problems with your scanner, check these things first.

Show a slide show using the Finder

Now that you have pictures available from the Finder, you can have your own, private slide show. It's easy: just select the photos and use the Quick Look icon to start the show. We suggest a folder with pictures of your grandkids!

1 Open Finder, then open the Pictures folder.

2 While holding down the Command key, select various pictures.

3 Click the Quick Look icon.

4 Click Play to start and click Esc on the keyboard to stop.

HOT TIP: The icon that offers the two diagonal arrows lets you view the slide show in full-screen mode.

HOT TIP: Copy your favourite pictures to a folder named Slide Show (you'll learn how to create folders and copy pictures later in this chapter) and when you want to watch a slide show of those photos, simply choose that folder and then follow the steps here.

Rename a picture

One of the first things you'll notice, both in this chapter and at your own computer, is that most of the pictures you'll see need new names. The generic names you see are created automatically by the camera, based on the date they were taken, among other things.

1 Choose a photo to rename. Select it by clicking it once.

2 Click once more on the current name of the file so that you see what's shown here.

3 Type the new name, taking care to keep the file extension (often .JPG).

4 Click Enter on the keyboard.

100_0584.JPG

3

Sheep.JPG

Organise pictures into folders

It's possible that you've imported, copied and scanned quite a few pictures by now, and that those pictures are all stored in the Pictures folder (and not organised into subfolders). This can make for an unwieldy group of pictures! But don't worry: you can create folders to organise your pictures quickly.

1 Open the Pictures folder.

2 Click the Settings icon and click New Folder.

3 Type a name for the folder.

4 Repeat.

5 After all folders are created, drag pictures into those folders as applicable.

? DID YOU KNOW?
If you decide to, you can drag an entire folder into another folder and make it a subfolder.

HOT TIP: Think about the subject matter of the pictures you keep. Now decide on some folder names to hold them. You may decide to create folders named Travel, Kids, Grandkids, Pets, Friends, among others.

HOT TIP: If a folder you create deserves its own subfolders, create them. For instance, in your Travel folder you may want to create subfolders for each place you've visited (Italy, Germany, the US, etc.).

Open a picture in Preview

Preview is an application that comes with your Mac which lets you view pictures. You can also perform basic tasks such as cropping, copying and adjusting the picture size. You can rotate an image and flip it, too, among other things.

1 Open Finder, click your user name and open the Pictures folder.

2 Open any picture. By default, Preview opens.

3 Explore each of the menu options. Tools>Flip Horizontal is shown here.

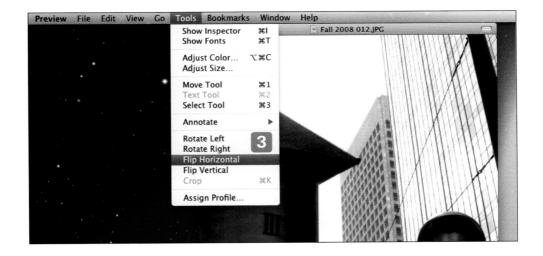

DID YOU KNOW?
You can view PDF files using Preview, and access basic tools such as Find, Spelling and Speech from the Edit menu.

 HOT TIP: To zoom in or out of a photo while using Preview, use the keyboard shortcuts Command + and Command −.

DID YOU KNOW?
When in any application, you can click and drag using the title bar to move the window to another area of the screen.

Crop a picture with Preview

When you crop a photo, you remove parts of the photo you don't want. As an example, in the photo here we'd like to keep the cat and lose as much of the shower mat as possible.

1 Open the photo to crop.

2 Click once inside the photo.

3 Click, hold and drag the cursor, now a + sign, around the area of the photo you want to keep.

4 Hold down the Command key and press the K on the keyboard.

5 To save your changes, click File>Save, or Command + S.

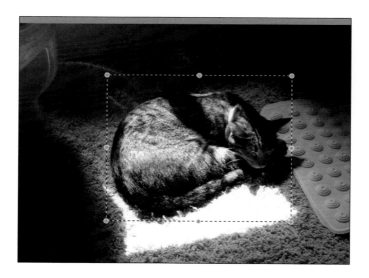

HOT TIP: If you save changes and decide later you don't want them, click File and click Revert to Saved.

HOT TIP: If you do not want to save the changes to the original file, click File>Save As. Name the file something else (perhaps Cat in Sun Spot Cropped).

? DID YOU KNOW?
If you don't crop out everything you want on the first attempt, you can crop again.

Rotate a picture with Preview

If you hold your camera sideways when you take a picture, it will appear sideways on your Mac after you import it. You'll need to rotate the photo to view it properly.

1 Open the Finder and select a photo.

2 Open it. It will open in Preview by default.

3 From the Menu bar, click Tools.

4 Choose Rotate Left or Rotate Right as desired.

5 To save the change, hold down the Command key and click the S.

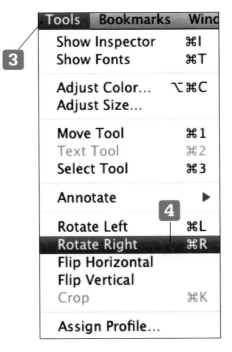

 HOT TIP: Explore all of the Menu bar options for Preview to get an idea of what's on offer.

 DID YOU KNOW?

You can set any picture as your Desktop picture from the Contextual menu (right-click, Settings icon, or Command + click).

Print with Preview

You can print your favourite pictures to share them with others when you're away from your computer. Print is an option from Preview's File menu, or you can use the keyboard shortcut Command + P.

1 Open a picture and verify that Preview is available on the Menu bar.

2 Click File>Print.

3 If you see only the small window, shown here, click the down arrow to see additional options.

4 Configure print options as desired.

5 Click Print.

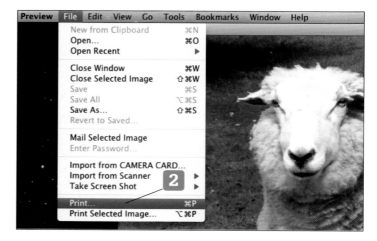

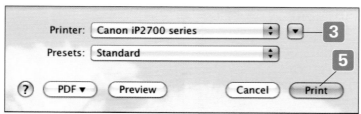

HOT TIP: Make sure you crop your photo before printing it.

HOT TIP: If you want to share a photo via email, click File and click Mail Selected Image. The image will be attached to a new email. All you have to do is add recipients, type a subject line and a bit of text, and you're ready to share!

DID YOU KNOW?

Some of the print options you may see include the ability to change the paper size, scale the image or print multiple copies.

Save a picture with Preview

Any pictures available from your Mac have already been 'saved' to it. However, you may still need to *resave* a picture to put it somewhere else, such as a networked computer or a USB stick. You may also need to save a picture if you're viewing one that's currently stored on some other device (a camera card, for instance) and that picture has not yet been saved to your Mac. Whatever the case, Preview offers a Save and a Save As option.

1 Open a picture in Preview.

2 Click File>Save As.

3 If applicable, click the arrow so you can see all of the options here.

4 Name the file.

5 Choose where to save the file.

6 Choose the desired format and quality. The defaults are often fine.

7 Click Save.

 HOT TIP: To locate the Pictures folder, click your user name in the left pane, then Pictures, and then any applicable subfolder.

WHAT DOES THIS MEAN?

Save As: Always offers first-time save options including the ability to name the picture and choose a place to save it. The Save command also offers first-time save options, but only the first time you use it. After that, Save simply saves changes you've made to the original file.

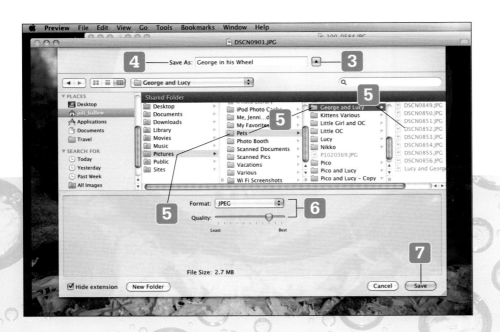

Open iPhoto and import pictures

iPhoto is available on the Dock (unless you've moved it) and also from the Applications window in the Finder. iPhoto offers much more than Preview does, and you can use it to create photo projects such as photo books and invitations, to sync your picture library with Facebook, and to sort your pictures by faces, events, albums, and more.

1 Open iPhoto from the Dock or the Applications window.

2 When prompted whether to open iPhoto when you connect your digital camera, click Decide Later.

3 To import photos into iPhoto:

    a. Click File>Import to Library.

    b. Browse to any picture folder to add.

    c. Click Import.

    d. Repeat as desired.

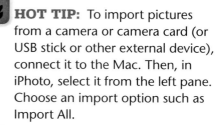

ALERT: We can't possibly introduce everything iPhoto has to offer here. However, Apple has created a video that will tempt you to learn more on your own. Visit www.apple.com/ilife/iphoto/ to view it.

HOT TIP: To import pictures from a camera or camera card (or USB stick or other external device), connect it to the Mac. Then, in iPhoto, select it from the left pane. Choose an import option such as Import All.

Explore iPhoto options

With pictures imported, you'll want to explore the iPhoto interface. You'll be surprised how much is available. Before you start, maximise the window by clicking the green + sign in the top left corner.

1 Click Events in the left pane. Review the titles listed.

2 Click Photos in the left pane to see all your photos.

? DID YOU KNOW?
You can click Search at the bottom of the iPhoto window to look for a photo using its name or other attributes.

ALERT: You may not have pictures in every Library folder listed in the left pane, or you may have more than you know what to do with, including duplicates! What you see will depend on your particular circumstances and will probably require some sorting out.

HOT TIP: In Events view, move your mouse over any Events folder and when you see your favourite picture appear, use Command + Click to access the contextual menu. Choose Make Key Photo from the options. The picture you set will be the 'cover' for that folder.

3 Click Faces, then:

   a. Click unnamed and type a name for each person shown.

   b. Click Show More Faces.

   c. Repeat as desired.

   d. Click Continue to Faces when you're ready.

4 Click Places, then:

   a. Hover your mouse over any pin.

   b. Click any item.

   c. Click Map to return (not shown).

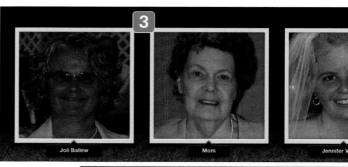

🔥 **HOT TIP:** Click Create at the bottom of the iPhoto interface to start a new project: Album, Book, Card, Calendar or Slideshow.

🔥 **HOT TIP:** If you need to increase the size of the thumbnails in, say, Events, Photos or Faces view, use the Zoom slider at the bottom of the iPhoto window.

Edit a picture with iPhoto

The Edit button is located at the bottom of the iPhoto window. When you click it, you have lots of options, including rotating the picture, enhancing it, fixing red-eye, straightening it, cropping it and retouching it. This makes editing pictures easy.

1 Select any photo to edit.

2 If you want iPhoto fix the photo automatically, click Enhance.

3 To straighten the picture, click Straighten.

4 To crop the photo, click Crop and drag from the corners, then click Done.

HOT TIP: When people are involved, click Fix Red-Eye and use your mouse to click inside the pupil and use the slider to set the size. Also, click Retouch to remove blemishes on a person's face or in another area of a photo.

HOT TIP: Click Effects and Adjust to see more iPhoto editing options. Boost, under Effects, often offers a colour improvement – if the photo has shadows, for instance.

Share pictures with others

With the perfect photo available, you may now be ready to share the photo with others. You have lots of share options: Order Prints, MobileMe Gallery, Flickr, Facebook or Email. Here, we'll opt to email a photo, but if you use Facebook or Flickr, feel free to give that a whirl, too.

1 Select a picture to email, or hold down the Command key while selecting multiple pictures.

2 Click Email.

3 Choose an option in the right pane, if you wish.

4 If you chose a theme in step 3, complete it by typing in your personal title, captions or a message.

5 Complete the email and click Send.

<table>
<tr><td>?</td><td>**DID YOU KNOW?**</td></tr>
</table>

DID YOU KNOW?
Do you see the Slideshow button at the bottom of the iPhoto window? Just select some photos and click it to view a slide show of them.

ALERT: Keep an eye on the email message size (in the bottom left corner of the email message). Anything over 4 MB might be rejected by your email server or your recipient's because it's too large.

9 Play, manage and obtain media

Introduction

Media is a broad term that is used to represent just about anything you can view, read or listen to. On your computer this can be music, home videos, movies and audiobooks. It can also be pictures, radio shows, podcasts, TV shows, even playlists of your favourite songs. You will acquire media from various sources, including your own music CD collection, which you can copy to your Mac, for free.

iTunes, included with all Apple OSes, is what you'll use to handle the media you acquire. iTunes offers access to the iTunes Store, too, where you can purchase media or rent movies, among other things. The iTunes Store is easy to navigate and it's equally easy to make purchases – we encourage you to explore it. Since iTunes is such a large part of the Mac-media experience, we'll start off this chapter with an overview of what you'll find there.

Update and explore iTunes

The very first time you open iTunes, you should check for updates first, then explore the options available from the Welcome screen. If you don't see the Welcome screen, it's easy to find it.

1 Open iTunes.

2 Click iTunes>Check for Updates. If updates are available, install them.

3 In the left pane of the iTunes Tutorials window, click Explore your iTunes Library. If you don't see this window:

   a. Click Help.

   b. Click iTunes Tutorials.

4 Explore other options as time allows.

🔥 **HOT TIP:** iTunes is available from the Dock by default, but if you've moved it it's also available from the Applications window in the Finder.

⚠️ **ALERT:** If this is your first time using iTunes, you may be prompted to work through some set-up screens. Just follow the prompts.

Listen to the radio

Hopefully you watched the tutorial in the iTunes Welcome screen as outlined in the previous section. If so, you know that you navigate iTunes by selecting an item in the left pane and that you then select the desired media from the right. This is how you listen to the radio.

1. In iTunes, click Radio in the left pane.

2. In the right pane, click any arrow to see the options.

3. Double-click any station to play it.

4. Click the Stop button to stop playing it.

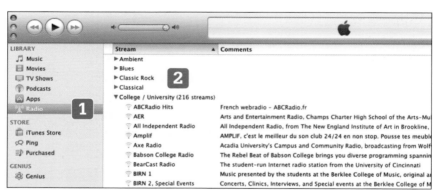

? DID YOU KNOW?

The radio stations you listen to in iTunes come to you via the Internet; they are not transmitted over the air and received through a radio antenna in the way you may be used to.

! ALERT: You must be connected to the Internet to listen to radio stations.

? DID YOU KNOW?

You can change the volume from inside the iTunes window (look to the right of the Stop button), from the Menu bar, from external speakers and, often, from media-compatible keyboards.

Play a music CD

When you insert a music CD into the CD drive on your Mac, iTunes will open and ask you if you want to *import* the songs that are on the CD into your iTunes library. Import is Mac-speak for copy. You may want to copy the CD, or you may simply want to listen to the songs on it.

1 Using the Finder or iTunes, make sure there's not a CD or DVD currently in the drive. If there is, click the Eject button (an up-facing arrow).

DEVICES

● Don McLean Classics ⏏

GENIUS **1**

2 Insert the music CD carefully, pushing slowly until the CD is accepted.

3 When prompted to import the CD, leave Do not ask me again deselected and click No.

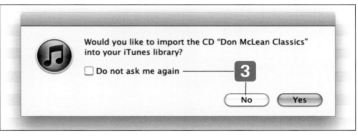

Would you like to import the CD "Don McLean Classics" into your iTunes library?

☐ Do not ask me again ——— **3**

(No) (Yes)

4 Click the CD in the left pane of iTunes.

5 Double-click any song in the list to play it.

6 When you're ready to eject the CD:

    a. Click the Eject button in iTunes, under Devices.

    or

    b. On the Desktop, drag the CD's icon to the Trash.

 HOT TIP: Use the controls that run across the top of the iTunes window to start a song again, pause a song or skip to the next song on the CD.

! ALERT: If you've been using iTunes for a while and have changed the preferences, you may not see the prompt shown here.

? DID YOU KNOW?
When one song in the list ends, the next one will begin automatically.

Copy songs from a CD

It's perfectly legal to copy songs from a CD you own to your Mac. This is known as 'ripping a CD', even though you aren't technically 'ripping off' anything. You may opt to rip your entire CD collection so that you can listen to music without inserting CDs, to create your own CDs that contain mixes of your favourite songs, to share the music with networked computers, or to copy those songs to other devices you own, such as an iPad or an iPhone.

1 Slowly insert a CD you'd like to copy.

2 If you see the prompt shown here, click Yes.

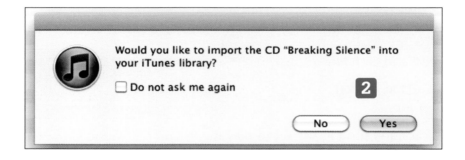

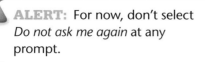

ALERT: For now, don't select *Do not ask me again* at any prompt.

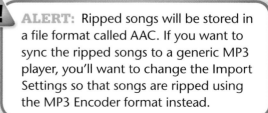

ALERT: Ripped songs will be stored in a file format called AAC. If you want to sync the ripped songs to a generic MP3 player, you'll want to change the Import Settings so that songs are ripped using the MP3 Encoder format instead.

3 Deselect any songs you don't want to copy.

4 Note that you can access Import Settings or Stop Importing from the iTunes window.

 HOT TIP: After your first CD is imported, you can access the songs from the Recently Added playlist near the bottom of the left pane in iTunes and the Music library.

? **DID YOU KNOW?**
During the import process, a green tick means the song imported successfully, a red X means it did not, and an orange squiggly line means it's still importing.

Create a playlist of music

If you've ever created a 'mixed tape' for an old boyfriend or girlfriend, you've created a playlist. A playlist is simply songs that, for whatever reason you deem appropriate, are grouped together. Once created, you can use the playlist to burn a CD or act as a DJ, among other things.

1 On the keyboard, click Command + N.

2 Type a name for the playlist.

3 Click Music in the left pane of iTunes.

4 Choose a view that enables you to see your music efficiently. We've chosen List View.

5 Drag any song to the new playlist to add it.

6 Repeat as desired.

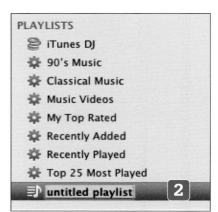

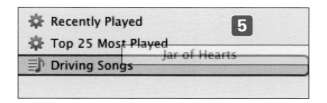

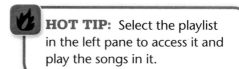

HOT TIP: Select the playlist in the left pane to access it and play the songs in it.

HOT TIP: Hold down the Command key to select multiple non-contiguous songs or the Shift key to select contiguous ones, then drag all the selected songs to a playlist in one move.

DID YOU KNOW?

When you add songs to a playlist you do not move them from their current location, you simply create a marker for the song in the new playlist.

Import media

If you set up a network as outlined in Chapter 5 and you have media on other networked computers you'd like to have on your Mac, you can import that media. If you have a lot of media, the process could take a few hours, though, so beware!

1 In iTunes, click File>Add to Library.

2 Browse to the location of the shared media.

3 Select the folder, perhaps Music or a subfolder in it, and click Choose.

4 Wait while the media imports.

5 If you see a new library in the left pane of iTunes, click it and note the related categories that appear across the top.

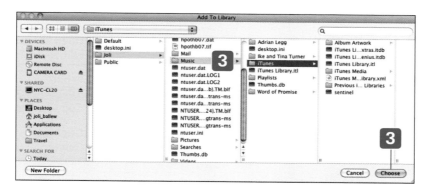

HOT TIP: You may be surprised at all of the media available to import from another computer to your Mac. For that reason, it's best to import small pieces at a time (your iTunes folder, for instance) rather than, say, importing all the media in your 'Users' folder.

ALERT: You can import music, audiobooks, movies and more, provided you have the proper rights, permissions and user names and passwords. You'll be prompted if a password is necessary.

Copy songs to a CD

You can copy music you own to a CD that you can listen to on your car or on a CD player. This is called 'burning a CD' because a laser actually burns the CD to write to it. It's legal to burn a CD for your personal use.

1 If there's a CD in the CD drive, eject it.

2 Insert a blank, writable CD.

3 If prompted, choose Open iTunes from the Action options and click OK.

4 Click the playlist to burn in the left pane and select the songs to burn to the CD.

5 Right-click the playlist and select Burn Playlist to Disc.

6 Review settings and click Burn.

	✔	Name	Time	Artist
1	✔	Jar of Hearts	4:07	Christina Perri
2	✔	Bad Day	3:54	Daniel Powter
3		Saving Grace (Theme)	3:08	Everlast
4		Welcome Me	4:36	Indigo Girls
5	✔	Jonas & Ezekial	4:08	Indigo Girls
6	✔	Ride Me Like A Wave	3:40	Janis Ian
7	✔	Tattoo	4:20	Janis Ian

 ALERT: If you decide not to burn the CD after all and can't find a way to eject it, restart your Mac and hold down the left mouse button (or trackpad if you have a laptop) as it boots up. Keep pressing it until the login screen or Desktop displays. The CD should eject.

 HOT TIP: A music CD that you can listen to in your car or CD player can hold about 80 minutes of music. You can see how many minutes you've allotted with selected songs at the bottom of the iTunes window.

 DID YOU KNOW?
If you purposefully select a playlist that's longer than 80 minutes, such as an audiobook, iTunes will span the media across multiple CDs, prompting you to input a new CD when the present one is full.

Play a movie on DVD

You can watch DVDs on your Mac, but you don't watch them in iTunes as you might expect – you watch them in DVD Player instead. Playing and watching a DVD is as simple as inserting it into the CD/DVD drive.

1 Insert the DVD into the CD/DVD drive on your Mac.

2 Wait while the DVD Player application opens.

3 To view the controls, move the mouse to the bottom of the screen.

4 Explore these controls:

    a. Click to see the DVD menu.

    b. Use to change the volume.

    c. Skip to previous chapter.

    d. Rewind.

    e. Pause/Play.

    f. Stop.

    g. Fast-forward.

    h. Skip to next chapter.

    i. Enable closed captioning (among other things).

    j. Eject.

    k. View options.

5 Right-click or Command + click on the movie screen to explore different views. Note the controls that appear in other modes.

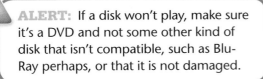**ALERT:** If you want to change modes to or from full screen, or to use half screen and other options, right-click the screen.

ALERT: If a disk won't play, make sure it's a DVD and not some other kind of disk that isn't compatible, such as Blu-Ray perhaps, or that it is not damaged.

? DID YOU KNOW?
The controls will be automatically hidden when in full-screen mode. In other modes, you'll have access to the controls all the time.

Download a free podcast

A podcast is often an informative lecture, news show, sermon or educational series offered free from colleges, news stations, churches and similar entities. You can browse free podcasts from the iTunes Store. If you find something you like, you can download a single podcast or subscribe to one to receive it on a schedule.

1 In iTunes, in the left pane, click iTunes Store.

2 Across the top of the iTunes window, click Podcasts.

3 Browse the podcasts as you'd browse a webpage, clicking links and using the Back button.

4 If you find a podcast you like and want to download:

    a. Click Free beside the podcast to download.

    b. Wait while the podcast downloads.

5 To listen to the podcast, click Podcasts in the left pane of iTunes.

6 Locate the podcast and click the Play icon.

? DID YOU KNOW?

Podcasts are also created by comedians, musicians and other entertainers to promote themselves, and sometimes even by companies touting a new product.

🔥 HOT TIP: When you subscribe to a podcast, it's downloaded automatically when a new podcast is available.

Listen to free iTunes U content

The iTunes Store offers a section called iTunes U. There you can access free lectures from colleges and universities all over the world. You browse the iTunes U store the same way you browse for podcasts; you listen to downloaded media in the same way, too.

1 In iTunes, click iTunes Store in the left pane.

2 Click iTunes U at the top of the iTunes window.

3 Browse what's on offer.

4 When you find something you like, click Free.

5 When the download completes, locate the item in the iTunes U section of iTunes to play it.

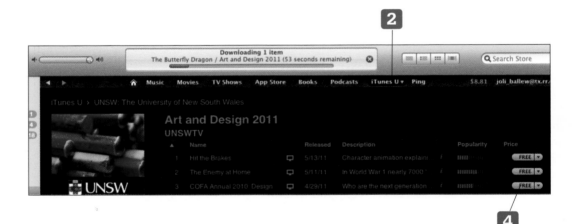

HOT TIP: Remember the Back button! It will take you to the previous page. If you ever get lost, though, just click iTunes U at the top of the iTunes window to start again.

DID YOU KNOW?

While browsing iTunes U, you can choose a category that interests you, such as Fine Arts, Literature or Social Science to narrow the results.

Buy media from the iTunes Store

The iTunes Store offers a lot of free media, as you've seen. You can also buy media. You may be interested in buying music or movies, for instance, but you can also buy TV shows, audiobooks, music videos and other items.

1 In iTunes, click iTunes Store in the left pane.

2 Browse the Music, Movies, TV Shows and Books options.

3 To buy something:

    a. Click the price or click Buy.

    b. Enter your Apple ID and password.

    c. Click Buy.

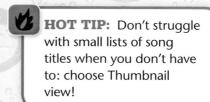

? **DID YOU KNOW?**

The App Store is an option in the iTunes Store. Apps are programs that can run on the iPhone, iPad and various iPods. If you have any i-devices, you can shop for apps from your Mac and sync them to your i-device later. Angry Birds is a very popular app and one you may have heard of – it's a game where you fling birds at objects to score points.

HOT TIP: Don't struggle with small lists of song titles when you don't have to: choose Thumbnail view!

4 In the left pane of iTunes, click Purchased.

5 Click to play the song or drag it to any playlist.

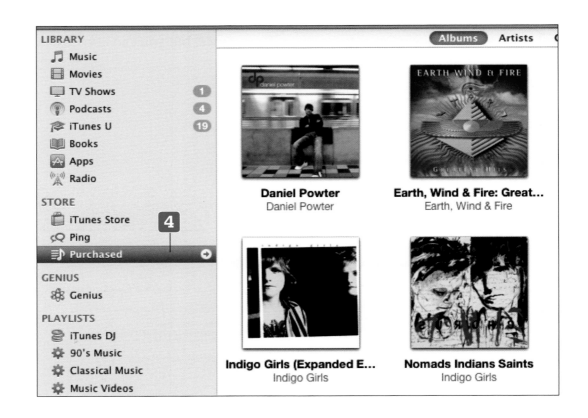

Create a Genius playlist

Genius is a feature of iTunes that will create a playlist for you, based on a single song you select. Genius will also suggest media you might like but don't yet own, by assessing the media you have and how often you listen to it.

1 In iTunes, in the left pane, click Genius.

2 Click Turn On Genius.

3 Type your password, agree to the terms of service and click Continue.

4 When Genius has completed its required tasks:

    a. Click Music in the left pane.

    b. Click your favourite song.

    c. Click the Genius icon at the bottom of the page.

5 The playlist will be created. Configure settings, or play or save the playlist, as you wish.

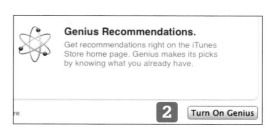

Genius Recommendations.
Get recommendations right on the iTunes Store home page. Genius makes its picks by knowing what you already have.

2 Turn On Genius

4c

Based On: **Bad Day by Daniel Powter** Limit to: (25 songs ⬧) (Refresh) (Save Playlist)

▲ ✔	Name		Time	Artist	Album	Genre	Rating	Pla
1	✔ Bad Day	(Ping ▼)	3:54	Daniel Powter	Daniel Powter	Rock	• • • • •	
2	✔ Don't Get Me Wrong		3:46	The Pretenders	Get Close	Rock		
3	✔ Sowing the Seeds of Love		6:19	Tears for Fears	The Seeds of Love	Alternative		
4	✔ Galileo		4:13	Indigo Girls	Rites of Passage (B...	Singer/Son...		
5	✔ What I Am		4:58	Edie Brickell & New...	Shooting Rubberba...	Alternative		

? **DID YOU KNOW?**
You can click Refresh to create a Genius playlist from the same starting song.

🔥 **HOT TIP:** In the right pane of iTunes, when a Genius playlist is selected, there are recommendations from the iTunes Store for similar media you might like.

⚠ **ALERT:** Some songs won't provide enough data for Genius to pull from and thus a Genius playlist will not be created. You'll be prompted if this is the case.

Share your media with others on your network

When you share the media on your Mac with others on your local network, people who have access to your Mac can also access the media on it. Sharing helps keep duplicates from being created across computers and lets you listen to the media that is on your Mac in other areas of the house.

1 From the Menu bar, click iTunes.

2 Click Preferences.

3 From the Preferences window, click the Sharing tab.

4 Tick Share my library on my local network.

5 Configure what to share, whether a password is required, and other options.

6 Click OK.

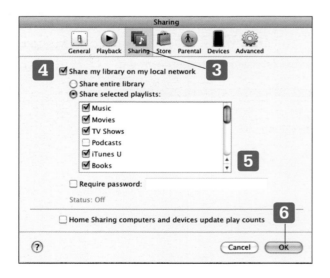

 HOT TIP: To protect children and grandchildren from accessing content that is not appropriate for them, either require a password or share only specific playlists.

? DID YOU KNOW?

Some of the playlists in iTunes are updated regularly to reflect your personal preferences. Top 25 Most Played is one of them. Your Mac counts how many times you play each song and adds songs here as they meet the *most played* threshold. If you don't want others who access your media on the network to count towards your play counts, do not tick Home Sharing computers and devices update play counts.

10 Secure and maintain your Mac

Back up with Time Machine

Time Machine is an application included with your Mac that lets you back up your data automatically. Time Machine keeps hourly backups for the past 24 hours, daily backups for the past month and weekly backups for the previous months until the disk you're backing up to is full. Then it writes over the oldest backups.

1 Open System Preferences>Time Machine.

2 Move the slider from Off to On.

3 Choose the external drive from the list of drives when prompted. (If you aren't prompted, click Select Disk.)

4 Click the disk and then click Use for Backup.

5 A backup will occur automatically.

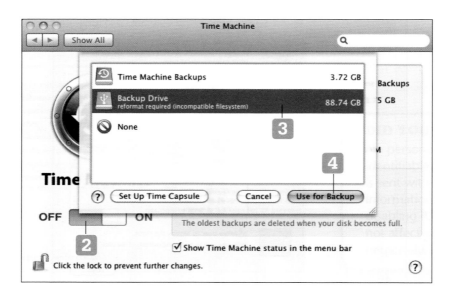

ALERT: You'll need an external backup device such as an external hard drive to get started with Time Machine. Ideally, it should be at least 160 GB.

ALERT: If you've prompted to erase what's currently on the drive, create a backup of it first on another computer if possible, or choose another backup device.

Set energy-saving options

Part of maintaining a Mac is to let it rest when you aren't using it. This is especially important for laptops running on battery power because it enhances battery life. It also lets both Desktops and laptops cool down, which is always good.

1 Open System Preferences>Energy Saver.

2 Use the sliders to set when the computer and the display sleep.

3 Configure other options as desired, noting that the defaults are generally fine.

4 To cause your Mac to start up, wake or sleep at a specific time:

a. Click Schedule.

b. Configure preferences as desired.

c. Click OK.

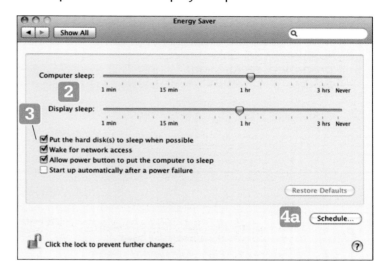

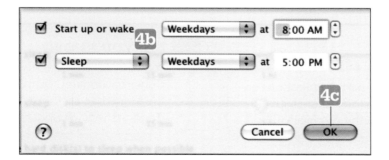

HOT TIP: Remember to click Show All after configuring any System Preferences to return to the System Preferences default screen.

DID YOU KNOW?

Computers use a lot of electricity. Configure all of the computers in your home or office to go to sleep on a schedule and you'll probably see improvements in your electricity bill.

Check for updates

Updates come in many forms. They can be updates to the operating system, updates to applications you've purchased, and updates to specific applications on your Mac, such as iTunes. Although your Mac will check for updates on a schedule, it's still a good idea to check for updates manually every now and then, just to be sure.

1 Click System Preferences>Software Update.

2 Click Check Now.

3 If new updates are available, click Continue to install them.

4 If prompted, restart your computer.

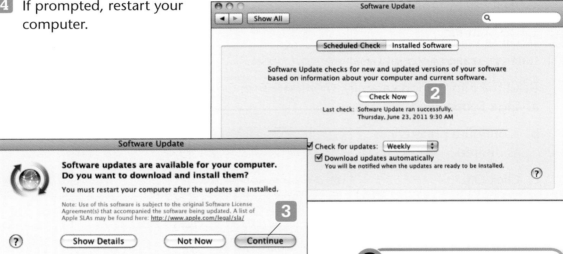

ALERT: If you have third-party applications on your Mac, open them and click File or Help and Check for Updates (or something similar).

 DID YOU KNOW?
You can also check iTunes for updates. From the Menu bar, click iTunes>Check for Updates.

HOT TIP: If you have an iPod, iPhone or iPad, connect it and check to see whether there are any updates for it, too.

HOT TIP: Sometimes Apple offers an update you can pay for, as with Lion, released in July 2011 for about £21. These updates offer many new features you would not otherwise have access to.

Encrypt with FileVault

FileVault encrypts the contents of your home folder. If your computer is stolen and a thief pulls the hard drive, he still won't be able to access your data without your password. You can turn on FileVault if you want the extra protection, but if you lose (or forget) your password, even you won't be able to access the data on it.

1 Click System Preferences>Security.

2 Click the FileVault tab.

3 Click Turn On FileVault.

4 Type a master password, verify it and type a hint only you can figure out.

5 Click Continue.

6 Enter your user account password and click OK.

7 Read the information carefully, then click Turn On FileVault (or click Cancel if you've changed your mind).

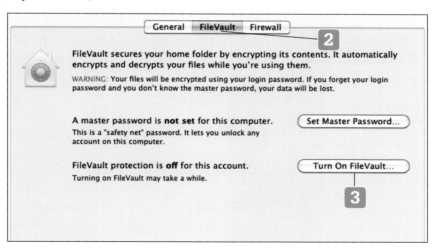

ALERT: You really need to write down your passwords and keep them somewhere, but that 'where' is the big issue. Consider storing your passwords in a locked safe if you have one. Even a locked filing cabinet or an unassuming shoe box in the wardrobe is better than nothing.

HOT TIP: Although this chapter is coming to an end, remember that common sense is the best way to protect and maintain your Mac. Make sure you read the next section carefully to lengthen the life of your Mac.

Use common sense to protect your Mac

There are lots of things you can do to protect you and your Mac that aren't available from System Preferences, such as ignoring email from people you don't know and logging off of your Mac when you've finished using it. But there are lots of other ways to protect your Mac you may not have thought of.

- Keep your laptop in your sight or locked up at all times.

- If you must leave a laptop in the car, make sure it's not too hot or cold, and that it's safely stored in the boot.

- Lock your home, hotel room, caravan or trailer every time you leave it, and if possible hide or physically lock down your Mac.

- Download software from reputable websites only and only after researching the software thoroughly.

- Protect external hard drives with encryption and passwords.

- Don't give your passwords to anyone, but do make them available to your children in your will or a safe deposit box they'll have access to should something happen to you.

- Back up data to your iPhone, iPad or iPod if you have one. Here, we're backing up our Music library (all 1,300+ songs).

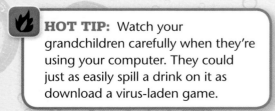

HOT TIP: Watch your grandchildren carefully when they're using your computer. They could just as easily spill a drink on it as download a virus-laden game.

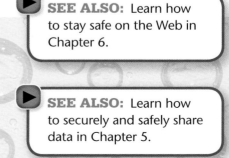

SEE ALSO: Learn how to stay safe on the Web in Chapter 6.

SEE ALSO: Learn how to securely and safely share data in Chapter 5.

11 Use and configure assistive technologies

Introduction

If you need assistance seeing what's on your Mac's screen, hearing the sounds it makes, using the keyboard or using the mouse, you can enable the applicable Universal Access technologies included with it. You can also make your Mac easier to use with features that aren't officially assistive technologies: you can change the screen resolution, purchase and connect a trackpad, use speech recognition, and more.

You don't need to have any audio, visual or tactile disabilities to enjoy these features, though. For instance, if you're sitting on the sofa with your keyboard and don't want to use a mouse, you can turn on Mouse Keys and use the numeric pad on your keyboard to control the cursor. You can use keyboard shortcuts to zoom in and out quickly instead of reaching for your reading glasses, or you can purchase and connect a trackpad to incorporate all kinds of new touch features built into the new Lion OS. This chapter is certainly worth exploring, no matter how young or old you are!

Learn how to use VoiceOver

VoiceOver will read text that appears on the screen to you. What it reads depends on how you configure the VoiceOver settings. Before you configure settings, though, turn on VoiceOver and work through the tutorial.

1 Open System Preferences>Universal Access.

2 Click the Seeing tab.

3 Under VoiceOver, Off is selected by default; click On.

4 Listen to the introduction, then press the space bar on the keyboard.

5 Work through the tutorial.

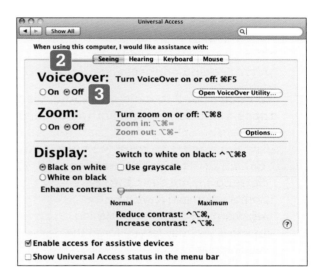

DID YOU KNOW?
The Option key on a PC keyboard is the Alt key. The Control key is the Windows key.

HOT TIP: To turn off VoiceOver, press Command + F5 (or the Windows key and F5).

HOT TIP: After working through the tutorial, click Open VoiceOver Utility and configure it with the settings you want.

Enable and use Zoom

Zoom lets you use a keyboard combination to enable Zoom and to zoom in and out. Once you get used to the commands, it's extremely easy (and convenient) to use this feature.

1 Open System Preferences>Universal Access.

2 From the Seeing tab, note the keyboard commands and try them now.

3 Click Options.

4 Set Maximum and Minimum Zoom.

5 Review the settings and click Done.

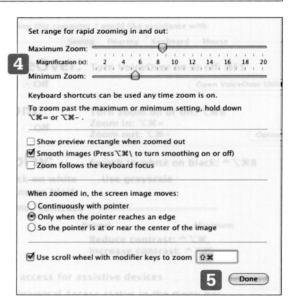

HOT TIP: Practise this several times now, write down the key combination and leave it by the keyboard. It's a very helpful thing to know and may let you forgo the reading glasses!

WHAT DOES THIS MEAN?

Zoom: With a Mac keyboard you turn on Zoom by holding down the Option and Command and 8 keys together; zoom in with Option and Command and = keys together; zoom out with Option and Command and – keys together. Press as many times as necessary to zoom in and out effectively.

Zoom: With a Windows keyboard you turn on Zoom by holding down the Alt and Windows and 8 keys together; zoom in with Alt and Windows and = keys together; zoom out with Alt and Windows and – keys together. Press as many times as necessary to zoom in and out effectively.

Switch to white on black display

You may have trouble seeing the typical black text on a white background display. If that's the case you can try its opposite, white on black. It is indeed the norm's polar opposite. When you make the change, the Menu bar and all menus will change, too, as will other areas of your Mac's interface.

1 Open System Preferences>Universal Access.

2 From the Seeing tab, select White on black.

3 If you wish, use the slider to enhance the contrast.

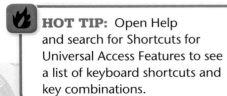

HOT TIP: Open Help and search for Shortcuts for Universal Access Features to see a list of keyboard shortcuts and key combinations.

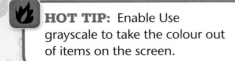

HOT TIP: Enable Use grayscale to take the colour out of items on the screen.

? DID YOU KNOW?

You can enable white on black with a key combination. For Mac keyboards, hold down the Control, Option, Command and 8 keys. For Windows keyboards, hold down the Ctrl, Windows, Alt and 8 keys.

Flash the screen when there's an audible alert

If you can't hear the sounds your Mac makes when there's an alert, you can tell your Mac to flash the screen when one occurs.

1 Click System Preferences>Universal Access.

2 Click the Hearing tab.

3 Place a tick beside Flash the screen when an alert sound occurs, and click Flash Screen to test.

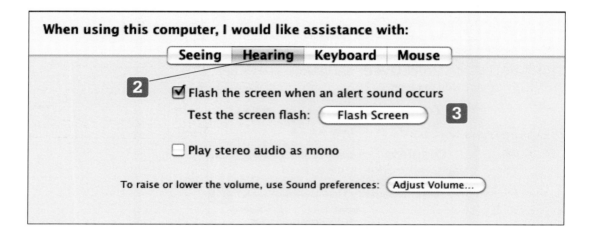

When using this computer, I would like assistance with:

Seeing **Hearing** Keyboard Mouse

2 ☑ Flash the screen when an alert sound occurs

Test the screen flash: (Flash Screen) **3**

☐ Play stereo audio as mono

To raise or lower the volume, use Sound preferences: (Adjust Volume...)

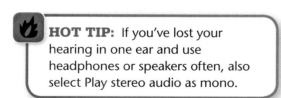

HOT TIP: If you've lost your hearing in one ear and use headphones or speakers often, also select Play stereo audio as mono.

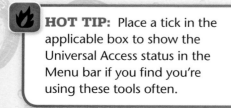

HOT TIP: Place a tick in the applicable box to show the Universal Access status in the Menu bar if you find you're using these tools often.

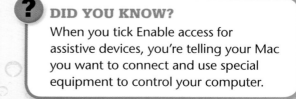

DID YOU KNOW?

When you tick Enable access for assistive devices, you're telling your Mac you want to connect and use special equipment to control your computer.

Make the keyboard easier to use

If you have trouble holding down three or four keyboard keys to perform a task, for instance holding down the Option, Command and 8 keys together to enable Zoom, you can turn on Sticky Keys. Once turned on, you could press the Option key, then the Command key and finally the 8 key (one at a time) to perform the command instead of holding down all the keys at the same time.

1 Open System Preferences>Universal Access.

2 From the Keyboard tab, enable Sticky Keys by clicking On.

3 If you wish, enable Press the Shift key five times to turn Sticky Keys on or off.

4 Explore other keyboard options.

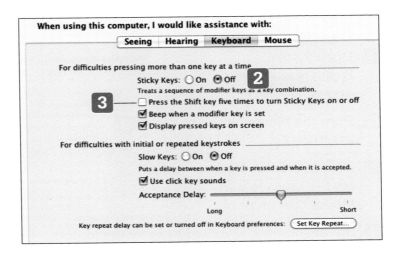

? **DID YOU KNOW?**

You can configure how long your Mac will wait before repeating a key you're pressing on the keyboard. To slow down the key rate (so that you have more time to press the key and remove your finger from it), click Set Key Repeat.

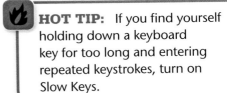 **HOT TIP:** If you find yourself holding down a keyboard key for too long and entering repeated keystrokes, turn on Slow Keys.

WHAT DOES THIS MEAN?

Sticky Keys: Lets you press a set of modifier keys as a sequence instead of all at once.

Use the keyboard in place of a mouse

You may have trouble using a mouse because your hands are too big, too small, have a tremor or are arthritic. You may simply have trouble reaching the mouse or have no place to put it. You can enable Mouse Keys to use your keyboard instead of your mouse if this is the case. Once enabled, you can use your keyboard or your numeric keypad to move the mouse.

1 Open System Preferences>Universal Access.

2 From the Mouse tab, next to Mouse Keys, click On.

3 Enable Press the Option key five times to turn Mouse Keys on or off.

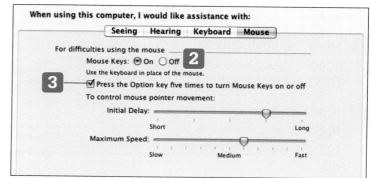

When using this computer, I would like assistance with:

Seeing Hearing Keyboard Mouse

For difficulties using the mouse
Mouse Keys: ● On ○ Off **2**
Use the keyboard in place of the mouse.
3 ☑ Press the Option key five times to turn Mouse Keys on or off
To control mouse pointer movement:
Initial Delay: ──────────────────
Short   Long
Maximum Speed: ──────────────────
Slow   Medium   Fast

4 Use the numeric keyboard to move the mouse:

a. Press 8 to move the cursor up.

b. Press 2 to move the cursor down.

c. Press 4 or 6 to move the cursor left or right.

d. Press 7, 9, 1 and 3 to move the mouse diagonally.

e. Press 5 to press the mouse button, 0 to hold the mouse button, and the period (full stop) to release the mouse button.

ALERT: If your computer doesn't have a numeric keypad, the following keys may have the numbers in parentheses printed on them: U (4), I (5), O (6), J (1), K (2), L (3) and M (0). Press the Fn key as you press these letter keys to use them as numeric keypad keys.

HOT TIP: Configure mouse options so that you can press the Option key on a Mac keyboard or the Alt key on a Windows keyboard five times to enable or disable Mouse Keys.

Increase the cursor size

The mouse cursor is pretty small. If you have trouble seeing the cursor, you can enlarge it. You can make it pretty large!

1 Open System Preferences>Universal Access.

2 Click the Mouse button.

3 Move the slider for Cursor Size until the cursor is the size you want.

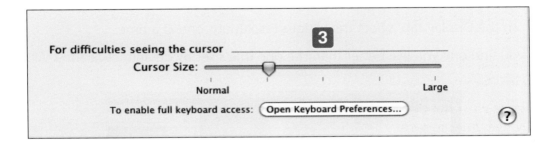

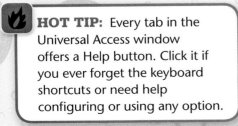

HOT TIP: Change the maximum speed of the mouse pointer movement to make it easier for you to use. We prefer a slower speed than the default, but you may prefer a faster one.

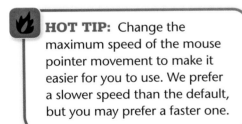

HOT TIP: Every tab in the Universal Access window offers a Help button. Click it if you ever forget the keyboard shortcuts or need help configuring or using any option.

DID YOU KNOW?
You can change the cursor size for your user account, and when your spouse or grandchild logs on with their own user account, the cursor and other settings will still be unique to them.

Change the screen resolution

The numbers that are shown in a screen resolution setting represent how many pixels make up the screen. If the screen resolution is 800 × 600, the screen is made up of 800 pixels across and 600 up and down. You should experiment with the settings and pick a resolution that's best for your eyes.

1 Open Finder, Safari and any other program you use regularly.

2 Position them on the screen so you can see at least part of each one.

3 Open System Preferences>Displays.

4 From the Display tab, select the various resolutions one at a time.

5 If you find one you like better than the one that's set by default, click Show All.

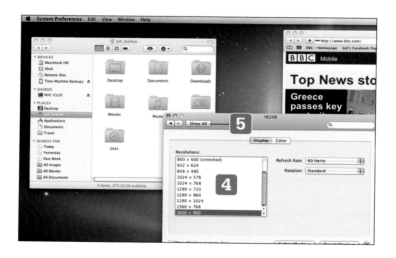

? DID YOU KNOW?
We can't tell you what resolution is best for you because how a resolution appears to you depends on your monitor size and type and your personal preferences.

HOT TIP: The lower the resolution, the larger everything appears on the screen.

WHAT DOES THIS MEAN?
Pixel: One square of colour data on a screen. More pixels mean a higher-quality image.

Use a trackpad

A trackpad, if you have one, lets you use gestures to zoom in and out, move items on the screen, and perform other tasks you'd normally do with the keyboard or mouse. We find that a trackpad is often easier for our over-50 readers to use, once they get used to it, because it takes many keyboard shortcut combinations (that are hard to remember) out of the picture. If you have a trackpad, try these techniques.

- Double-tap the trackpad to zoom in and out of a picture, webpage or any other screen element.

- Drag three fingers up and down to scroll through a webpage or list of items.

- Drag three fingers left and right to switch between full-screen apps.

- Pinch in and out with two fingers to zoom in or out.

- Swipe with two fingers to navigate webpages.

- Triple-drag up to see Mission Control (a Lion feature).

- Drag all fingers towards the centre to open Launchpad (a Lion feature).

- Configure your trackpad with your own preferences from System Preferences.

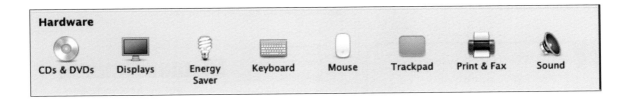

Hardware

CDs & DVDs | Displays | Energy Saver | Keyboard | Mouse | Trackpad | Print & Fax | Sound

HOT TIP: If you don't have a trackpad, you can buy one from Apple. Visit the Apple Store at store.apple.com.

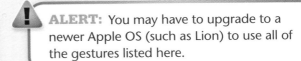

ALERT: You may have to upgrade to a newer Apple OS (such as Lion) to use all of the gestures listed here.

Give voice commands to your Mac

If you have a microphone installed and enable Speakable Items, you can speak various commands. One is 'What time is it?'; others include 'Get my mail' and 'Open my browser'. Your Mac will respond appropriately.

1 Open System Preferences>Speech.

2 Click the Speech Recognition tab and click On for Speakable Items.

3 Choose the microphone (or input device) you want to use.

4 Note the other options, then click Calibrate.

5 Speak the sample commands and verify that your microphone is working.

6 Click Done.

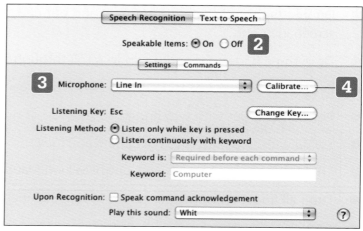

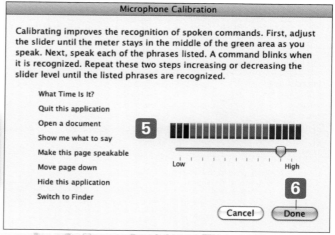

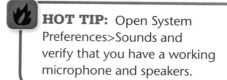

HOT TIP: Open System Preferences>Sounds and verify that you have a working microphone and speakers.

ALERT: If you don't see the meter move during the calibrating process, you will probably need to install a microphone. In other cases, while a webcam may show up as an option during calibration and work for audio in other instances, it may not work here for speakable commands.

7 Hold down the Esc key and speak a command.

8 Click the Commands tab.

9 Click Global Speakable Items, then click Configure.

10 If you wish, disable Speak command names exactly as written and click OK.

11 Click Open Speakable Items Folder.

12 Review the available commands.

 HOT TIP: When viewing the items in the Speakable Items folder, consider List view, as shown here.

 DID YOU KNOW?
'Tell me a joke' is a valid speakable command, as is 'What day is it?'

Have the clock announce the time

To protect your eyes, it's best to look away from the computer every hour or so and focus on something else for a few minutes. You can get your Mac to remind you to do that by configuring it to speak the time 'on the hour'.

1 Open System Preferences>Date & Time.

2 From the Clock tab, tick Announce the time.

3 Choose how often to announce the time.

4 Note you can choose a new system voice here, too, by clicking Customize Voice.

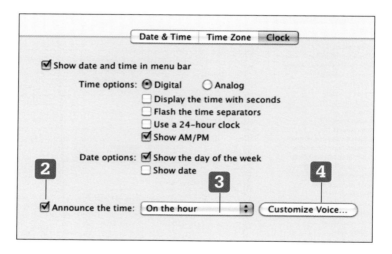

 HOT TIP: To return to the System Preferences options while in any other, click Show All.

? DID YOU KNOW? From the Date & Time options you can change the way the time appears on the Menu bar by clicking Analog, or by using a digital 24-hour clock, among other things.

HOT TIP: Opt to show the date in the Date & Time options. It will appear on the Menu bar.

Choose a new system voice

You may not like 'Alex', the default system voice. You may prefer Bruce, Fred, Kathy, Vicki or Victoria. And if you click Show More Voices, you'll have access to many more. Once you've selected a voice, you can test it to see whether you like it.

1 Open System Preferences>Speech.

2 Click the Text to Speech tab.

3 Next to System Voice, click the down arrow to see the options.

4 Select a voice or choose Show More Voices first.

5 Click Play.

6 Repeat as desired.

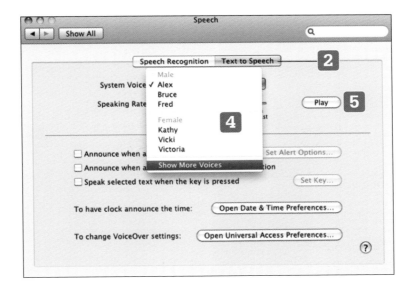

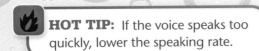

ALERT: If you can't hear the voice, turn up the volume on the Menu bar.

HOT TIP: If the voice speaks too quickly, lower the speaking rate.

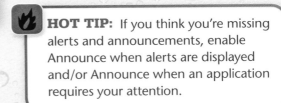

HOT TIP: If you think you're missing alerts and announcements, enable Announce when alerts are displayed and/or Announce when an application requires your attention.

Top 10 Mac Problems Solved

Problem 1: The items in the Finder window are too small for me to see

Often, the items you need to work with in a Finder window are simply too small to make out. If this is the case, try thumbnail view. In this view you can make folders appear larger using the zoom slider at the bottom of the Finder window. If your over-50 eyes are struggling to make out what's on the screen, this is the way to go.

1 Open Finder and click your user name in the Sidebar.

2 Verify that thumbnail view is selected.

3 Locate the slider in the bottom right corner and slide it towards the right.

4 If you're still having trouble making out what's on the screen, click the Quick Look icon.

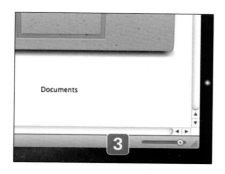

? DID YOU KNOW?

Ctrl + click (or right-click if applicable) will access the contextual menu for any folder. There you can make an alias for the folder, duplicate the folder, and more.

🔥 HOT TIP: There are views other than thumbnail view; however, the other views are harder to read because they're smaller and don't offer a zoom feature. We prefer thumbnail view so we don't have to put on our reading glasses!

Problem 2: My grandchild wants to use my Mac, but I want to keep my private data private

An easy way to share your Mac with others is to create a user account for them. Then they can log on to your computer using that account and access the data you've specifically shared, configure their own Desktop background and screen saver, and more. For grandkids, you can even set parental controls.

1 Open System Preferences.

2 Click Accounts.

3 If necessary, click the lock so that you can make changes.

4 Click the + sign just above the lock icon.

5 Fill in the required information for the new user and click Create Account.

6 Answer any additional prompts, as warranted.

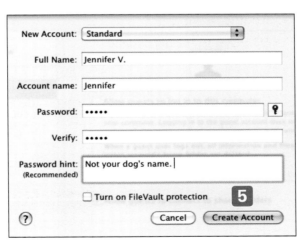

 DID YOU KNOW?
Parental controls is an option in System Preferences.

! ALERT: Create a user account for each user who will access your computer or the data on it. Make sure all accounts have passwords applied, even your grandchildren's accounts.

Problem 3: I've set up a network but can't access a Windows computer that's on it

You may have to 'mount' computers before you can access them. If you've created a network, joined a workgroup and feel the rest is in order, try this to access other computers you should have access to.

1 Open the Finder.

2 From the Menu bar, click Go.

3 Click Connect to Server.

4 Keep **smb://** and replace the rest with the name of the Windows computer you want to connect to.

5 Click the + sign to add the server to your list of Favorite Servers.

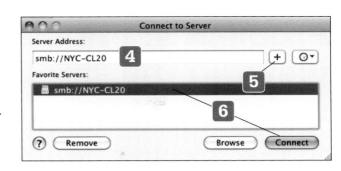

6 Select the server in the list and click Connect.

7 Input the administrator name and password used on the Windows computer.

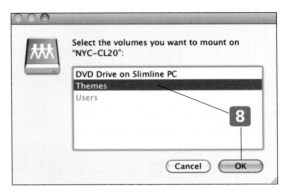

8 Select the folder to connect to and click OK.

9 An icon for the Windows computer will appear in the Finder. Click it to see the shared folders.

⚠️ **ALERT:** Unless you specify otherwise in Accounts, under the tab Login Items, you'll have to mount the server after every reboot of your Mac.

❓ **DID YOU KNOW?**
You can delete a server from the Favorite Servers list by clicking the server and clicking Remove.

Problem 4: I'm having trouble viewing the small print on a webpage

If you have trouble viewing search results or what's on a webpage, you can zoom in on it. This will make everything on the page larger. It may be just what your aching over-50 eyes have been searching for! There are two ways to zoom in on a page:

- Hold down the command key (or the Windows key if applicable) and press the + sign. Repeat as often as you need to. (Press Command and – to zoom back out.)

Safari	File	Edit	**View**	History	Bookmarks	W

Hide Toolbar	⌘ |
Customize Toolbar...	
Hide Bookmarks Bar	⇧⌘B
Show Tab Bar	⇧⌘T
Show Status Bar	⌘ /
Stop	⌘.
Reload Page	⌘R
Actual Size	⌘0
Zoom In	⌘+
Zoom Out	⌘—
Zoom Text Only	

- Click View, then click Zoom In. This will zoom in on everything, including images.

 ALERT: By default, when you zoom in on a page, you'll zoom in on the images, too. Sometimes they'll distort, but often you don't need to zoom in on the images anyway, only the text. If you want to change the default so that the Zoom command increases the text size only, click View and click Zoom Text Only.

 HOT TIP: If you're still having trouble viewing what Safari has to offer, try Window>Zoom from the Menu bar.

 HOT TIP: Make sure the Safari window is maximised and drag to enlarge the window even more from the bottom right corner of Safari to make the window as large as possible.

? **DID YOU KNOW?**
We like the Bookmark bar, but you can hide it if you wish. This will increase Safari's screen size a little. Choose Hide Bookmarks Bar from the View menu to do this.

Problem 5: I don't know how to stay safe on the Web

Although Safari will warn you when you try to access a fraudulent website (one that's been reported, anyway), prompt you to verify you want to send secured information away from a secure website when applicable, and block pop-up ads, among other things, you still have to be very careful when surfing the web. Here are a few things to remember:

- If you are prompted by your Mac to input a password while surfing the Web, think twice. This means you're about to download something and downloads can contain viruses and other harmful code.

- When inputting credit card information, make sure the address in the Address bar starts with https://. That means it's secure.

- Don't give your login name and password to an application (such as one you might find on Facebook) unless you've researched it and determined the application is safe. (Many are; many are not.)

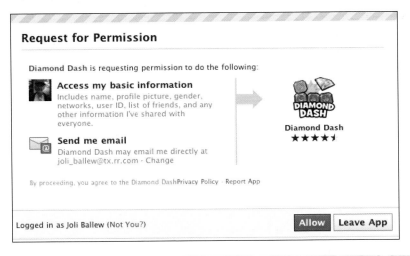

 HOT TIP: When you're finished using Safari, for good measure, click Safari and click Quit Safari.

 ALERT: If you let others use your computer with your login name, they can easily send email as you, update your social status, download harmful content, and more. It's best to create user accounts for others who can use your computer and log out when you aren't using it yourself.

Problem 6: I have tried to configure an email account in Mail, but I keep getting errors

Sometimes when you add an account, Mail can't configure it automatically and asks you to input additional information. If you see the prompt here, choose to set up your email account manually. When you do this, it's important to note that you must input the information exactly as provided by your ISP or you'll encounter errors.

1 If prompted during account set-up, click Setup Manually.

2 Leave POP selected unless you're positive you need to select something else.

3 Fill in the required information. You will probably have to contact your ISP.

4 Click Continue.

5 Continue working through the screens offered. What you see and input will differ depending on your email provider's requirements.

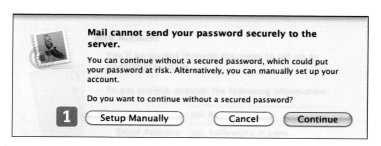

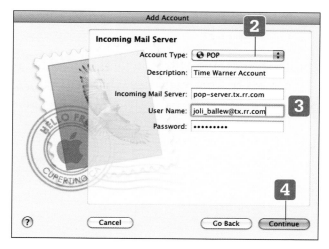

Problem 7: I can't seem to copy pictures from my digital camera to my Mac

If you have a digital camera you can copy the pictures on it to your Mac. If your camera isn't recognised, though, or you can't access it for some other reason, you can use the digital camera's SD card instead.

1 Remove the camera card from the camera and insert it into your Mac's card reader.

2 Open Finder and select the device.

3 If applicable, open any folders and subfolders necessary to access the pictures.

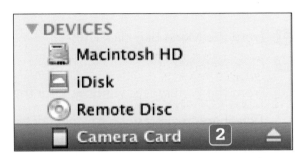

4 To select all the pictures in a folder, click Edit>Select All.

5 To select some of the pictures in a folder, hold down the Command key while selecting.

6 Click Edit>Copy Items.

7 Open the Pictures folder and click Edit>Paste Items.

? **DID YOU KNOW?**

If your Mac isn't compatible with the type of camera card your camera uses, consider purchasing a USB card reader. They're often fairly inexpensive.

? **DID YOU KNOW?**

The keyboard shortcut for Copy is Command + C; the keyboard shortcut for Paste is Command + V.

HOT TIP: If you like to drag and drop, open the Pictures window and the Device window. Then you can drag files from the device to the open folder instead of using Copy and Paste.

Problem 8: I can't access the media on my Mac from other networked devices

When you share the media on your Mac with others on your local network, people who have access to your Mac can also access the media on it, as can devices. Sharing helps keep duplicates from being created across computers and lets you listen to the media that is on your Mac in other areas of the house.

1 From the Menu bar, click iTunes.

2 Click Preferences.

3 From the Preferences window, click the Sharing tab.

4 Tick Share my library on my local network.

5 Configure what to share, whether a password is required, and other options.

6 Click OK.

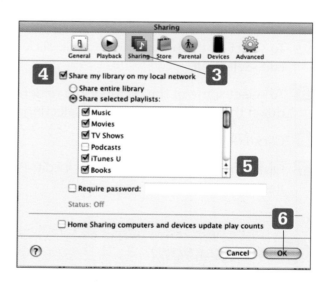

> **HOT TIP:** To protect children and grandchildren from accessing content that is not appropriate for them, either require a password or share only specific playlists.

? DID YOU KNOW?

Some of the playlists in iTunes are updated regularly to reflect your personal preferences. Top 25 Most Played is one of them. Your Mac counts how many times you play each song and adds songs here as they meet the *most played* threshold. If you don't want others who access your media on the network to count toward your play counts, do not check Home Sharing computers and devices update play counts..

Problem 9: Family members are using my Mac when I'm not around

The best way to secure your Mac from access by your kids, grandchildren or spouse is to protect it with a strong password. Once it's protected, you can enhance that security by logging off automatically after a specific period of time or configuring a password-protected screen saver.

1 Open System Preferences and click Accounts.

2 For every account that does not have a password (or a strong password), click either Change Password or Reset Password, as applicable.

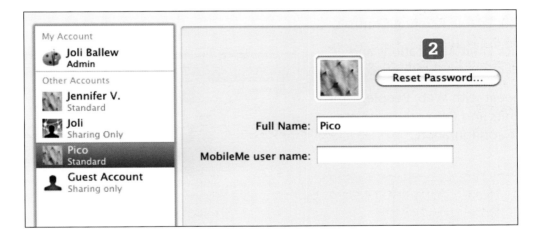

3 Type the new password twice, and type a password hint.

4 Click Reset Password.

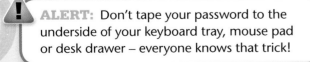 **ALERT:** Don't tape your password to the underside of your keyboard tray, mouse pad or desk drawer – everyone knows that trick!

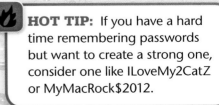 **HOT TIP:** If you have a hard time remembering passwords but want to create a strong one, consider one like ILoveMy2CatZ or MyMacRock$2012.

Problem 10: I don't want my grandchildren using the computer after a certain time of day

If you have grandchildren who use your Mac when they visit, you can enable parental controls. With this feature you can display a simple Finder, limit what applications they can use (including access to the App Store) and even prevent them from making changes to the Dock. Logs are available to monitor their activities, too.

1 Open System Preferences>Parental Controls.

2 Click the user account to configure (it must be a 'Standard' account).

3 Click Enable Parental Controls.

4 Click Limit Applications and select the applications to allow.

5 Repeat with Web, People, Time Limits and Other to complete the configuration.

Parental Controls

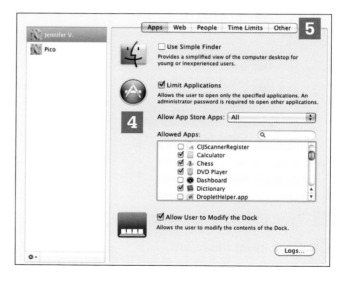

 **HOT TIP:** When configuring parental controls, under Time Limits, set a bedtime for both school nights and weekends for each grandchild. This will limit their computer use when you're not watching them.

? DID YOU KNOW?
Parental Controls offers a People tab that lets you state who your child or grandchild can communicate with. If you like, you can limit it to their parents and siblings, and perhaps a best friend or two.